ARMS IN THE INDIAN OCEAN:
Interests and Challenges

THE INDIAN OCEAN REGION

ARMS IN THE INDIAN OCEAN:

Interests and Challenges

Dale R. Tahtinen
With the assistance of
John Lenczowski

American Enterprise Institute for Public Policy Research
Washington, D.C.

Dale R. Tahtinen is the assistant director of foreign and defense policy studies at the American Enterprise Institute.

John Lenczowski is a research assistant at AEI.

AEI Studies 145

Library of Congress Cataloging in Publication Data

Tahtinen, Dale R
    Arms in the Indian Ocean.

    (AEI studies ; 145)
    1. United States—Military policy. 2. Russia—
Military policy. 3. Indian Ocean region—Politics and
government. I. Lenczowski, John, joint author. II. Ti-
tle. III. Series: American Enterprise Institute for
Public Policy Research. AEI studies ; 145.
UA23.T26   355.03'30182'4   77-1548
ISBN 0-8447-3242-7

Printed in the United States of America

CONTENTS

INTRODUCTION

Historically, the Indian Ocean has commanded strategic importance, especially since Vasco da Gama's landing in India at the end of the fifteenth century. At that time, spices were the valuable resource sought from the Near East and South Asia. During the following centuries many other products made their way across the Indian Ocean toward Europe, the United States, Japan, and elsewhere. The best known and most important commodity crossing these waters today is petroleum—the "black gold" used to run industries and heat homes in nearly every industrialized country of the West.

Particularly since Great Britain announced its intent to withdraw from "east of Suez" in 1968, there has been a flurry of interest by other major powers and by the Indian Ocean littoral states themselves over which of them, if any, shall become the dominant influence in this key region. There is one certainty: the Indian Ocean will no longer be a British lake. Some observers contend that no one state will ever again dominate this ocean, the third largest in the world.

During the last several years, various states have engaged in activities bearing on the future of the Indian Ocean. These actions, by both outside powers and nations indigenous to the area, have resulted in a significant increase in the quality and quantity of military equipment in the ocean region.

This study will assess both the military strength of the littoral states and the military presence of external powers, though the use of highly debatable statistics such as ship days will be avoided. An effort will also be made to identify the conflicts that could erupt in the region. Overall, it is hoped that, by discussing these related topics, the future role of the United States in this vitally important and sensitive area of the world will be clarified. Much has already been written about the pros and cons of U.S. policy options concerning the Indian Ocean, but even more study is needed of an area that could easily become the scene of another superpower arms race. Any such competition between the Soviet Union and the United States would, of course, carry with it the danger of a confrontation that could conceivably lead to thermonuclear war.

1

THE MILITARY POSITION
OF THE REGIONAL STATES
AND SOME OUTSIDE POWERS

Strength of Littoral States

It has not been uncommon in recent years to hear or read about the "power vacuum" left in the Indian Ocean in the wake of the British withdrawal.[1] Consequently, it is important to consider how much military power is now held by the Indian Ocean littoral countries. One of the best ways to do this is to determine their present air, army, and naval strengths and the likelihood of their expanding these elements of military power in the future. In this connection, it is interesting to trace the patterns of weapons acquisitions during the years since London's historic announcement.

Air strength can be considered first. The littoral states have already amassed a rough total of some 2,600 combat aircraft. Although the radius of many of these planes is limited to several hundred miles, their use could influence developments in the region. For instance, many of the Indian Ocean states could at least defend their territorial waters against hostile intrusion by limited military forces, and a number of them could also protect fishing and mineral resources from exploitation. Despite the limited range of their aircraft, they could also probably protect their territorial waters up to the 200-mile-wide fishing and mineral exploitation zones that are soon likely to be declared by many countries. A combination of naval craft and air power can be a potent means of enforcing such claims.

---

[1] For purposes of this study, the term *Indian Ocean states* includes all those countries littoral to that body of water and its appendages, such as the Persian Gulf, the Arabian, Red, and Andaman Seas, the Bay of Bengal, the Gulfs of Aden and Oman, and the Mozambique Channel. In the discussion of the strength of the littoral nations, however, none of the Red Sea powers northwest of Ethiopia and Saudi Arabia is included, but these powers are mentioned in connection with possible conflicts in the Strait of Bab el Mandeb.

Specifically, Australia, South Africa, Indonesia, India, Pakistan, and the three major Persian Gulf states of Iran, Iraq, and Saudi Arabia are most capable of protecting their respective interests by means of air power. Indeed, most of these countries have enough air strength to prevent their takeover by all but the major powers. As will be noted, however, this strength will not necessarily prevent armed conflicts from arising.

The most effective long-range air forces are those of Australia, which possesses F-111Cs and A-4s, and of Iran, whose F-4 Phantoms and newly acquired F-14s are the most sophisticated of all the aircraft held by Indian Ocean states. Even the F-4s are more advanced than most of the planes in the region, and the expected delivery of some 160 F-16 fighters will further modernize and strengthen Iran's military establishment.

Both the Australians and the Iranians are also adding the highly sophisticated P-3 Orion aircraft to their inventories. With a maximum mission radius of over 2,000 nautical miles and an ordnance load of over nine tons, these planes will markedly increase the long-range surface surveillance and antisubmarine warfare capabilities of both countries. The air forces of India, Pakistan, and South Africa are similar in composition to those of Australia and Iran but lack the extensive range made possible by the P-3 Orion. Nevertheless, these three countries still maintain a respectable level of air power.

In general, as reflected in Table A-1, a significant number of the region's states possess relatively modern aircraft that can be used in an antishipping or antinaval role. Included in their inventories are various versions of aircraft, such as the A-4, F-5, Mirage III and V, and MiG-21 and 23. When in-flight refueling is possible, the operational combat radius can obviously be increased many fold.

Although quality and, to a somewhat lesser extent, quantity of combat aircraft are important, the human factor plays a paramount role. It is essential, therefore, to consider not only whether pilots can effectively use the available equipment but also whether maintenance crews can keep the maximum number of aircraft and associated avionics ready for combat. In regard to the latter, one must also take into account turnaround times (the time it takes to refuel and reload a plane) in order to estimate the number of sorties each force can make in a combat situation. Of the Indian Ocean nations, Australia, India, Iran, Pakistan, and South Africa produce the best qualified and trained combat crews for both air and ground operations.

However, it should be noted that evaluation of the human element is often difficult. Usually it can be fairly assessed only with a thorough understanding of the culture and character of a given nation. An analysis of national character and of corollary matters such as national martial traditions is beyond the scope of this study. The extent and efficacy of the economic infrastructure of a given country, however, is often a good barometer of its military efficiency.

Using this criterion, it is not surprising that countries like South Africa and Australia, which have comparatively well-developed economic infrastructures, are capable of producing efficient maintenance crews and aircraft auxiliary supply and back-up facilities. The same is true of India, which has developed a considerable infrastructure, including an indigenous arms industry, but the nation suffers from many internal problems and has gross differences in the cultural backgrounds of the various segments of its population. India generally recruits its armed forces from its elite literate classes, thereby avoiding the inherent deficiencies of armies composed of less educated personnel.

Pakistan, perhaps the poorest of the main military powers in the region, has the least extensive infrastructure. Nevertheless, with a history of considerable combat experience and active participation in CENTO military affairs, the Pakistanis have produced, for example, some of the best pilots in the region. Indeed, Pakistani pilots have been sent to Iran, Iraq, and some other Arab countries to train their air forces.

Iran is a very different case. Devoid of any modern infrastructure until recently, Iran is now using its vast oil revenues in an attempt to build one with great rapidity. However, there remains a large shortage of trained personnel at all levels—from semiskilled labor to middle management—and the Iranian military has virtually no combat experience except that gained from its participation in fighting the Dhofar rebels in Oman. Nevertheless, the Iranian air force has been evaluated as logistically effective, and some American military sources even see it as being more effective than that of Pakistan and as having pilots more disciplined than those of Israel.[2]

Another element of air power with particular relevance to the Indian Ocean is the helicopter. Once air superiority is achieved, helicopters can provide critical tactical air mobility for men and materiel, either during full-scale warfare or in counterinsurgency situations. They are also crucial in the tactical zone for inserting long-

---

[2] Drew Middleton, "Despite Huge Outlays, Iran's Forces Are Short of Security Aims," New York Times, July 14, 1975. Also see Eric Pace, "Iran's Vast Purchases of Weaponry Strain Ability of Country to Absorb It All," New York Times, January 5, 1976.

range combat/reconnaissance teams behind enemy lines, and for serving as highly effective gunships against personnel and armor.

For many of the Indian Ocean littoral states, helicopters, like combat planes, can be used for close-in patrol of territorial waters. Depending upon their weapons configuration, they can also be utilized in an antishipping role, challenging both submarines and a variety of armed surface vessels. Obviously, this airborne potential could easily be used against merchant shipping or any other non-military activity within the claimed waters of a state.

Without a doubt, the more than 800 helicopters in the hands of Indian Ocean states can directly contribute to the needs of those states. The interest shown by many of them in procuring ever greater numbers of helicopters reflects the importance placed on them. Indeed, the fact that major powers such as the United States, the Soviet Union, Britain, and France produce helicopter carriers indicates the critical naval role these rotary aircraft can assume. In addition to their value for reconnaissance or in actual combat situations, helicopters can make a significant contribution to sea-related electronic warfare.

Notwithstanding the usefulness of combat planes and helicopters, in order to be most sucessful, a naval defensive or offensive force must include a variety of surface and subsurface vessels and associated weapon systems. With or without a high degree of air cover or a unified air-surface capability, a small nation can wreak a considerable amount of damage on the seaborne ships of other states with a force consisting of submarines and/or fast, missile-armed patrol craft. The powerful missiles can incapacitate or even destroy much larger ships with relative ease, while the craft themselves make an elusive target because of their size and speed. Little needs to be said about the warfare potential of larger ships like frigates and destroyers with modern surface-to-surface missiles, antisubmarine equipment, and even surface-to-air capabilities.

India boasts the most impressive fleet in the region with twenty-three frigates, two cruisers, three destroyers, eight submarines, and one aircraft carrier. The carrier complement includes both strike and antisubmarine aircraft and would undoubtedly be a prime target of a hostile force. As long as it remains operational, however, its aircraft would threaten with elimination any enemy force operating within their combat radius.

The Indian navy will become even more formidable when current plans to enlarge its forces are implemented. India will reportedly acquire three Leander-class frigates (Avisos), which are designed basically for antisubmarine warfare, but would also probably be

4

equipped with Exocet surface-to-surface missiles.[3] The Avisos have a 4,500-mile range at a speed of some fifteen knots.[4] The Indian buildup allegedly includes an order from the Soviet Union for eight Nanuchka-class, missile-armed corvettes, which are said to have been built for protecting coastal waters but would seem to be suited for patrolling well beyond claimed territorial limits.[5] The Indians also intend to fit their Leander-class frigates with their own surface-to-surface missiles and to acquire better long-range, but unnamed, anti-submarine missiles. Finally, India's aircraft carrier will be modernized and its Sea Hawk planes replaced by new multimission aircraft, presumably of either Soviet or British manufacture.[6]

Indicative of India's expanding military operations has been the proposed plan for the strategically located Nicobar Islands in the Bay of Bengal near the straits of Malacca. New Delhi has appropriated some $49 million to construct a so-called export-processing zone in these unexploited islands. Since the Nicobars are considered unsuitable for economic development, the Indian plan has been looked upon as a pretext for the construction of an airfield and a maritime infrastructure, which could be used as a base for Indian military operations.[7]

In the future India will most likely find that its major competitor for naval quality and size is Iran, which has embarked upon an ambitious modernization program. Iran's navy is scheduled over the next several years to receive at least four American-made Spruance-class destroyers, the most modern, and probably the best, ever developed. In addition, Iran has reportedly ordered three Tang-class submarines [8] and made inquiries about procuring an aircraft carrier.[9]

---

[3] "International Defense Digest," *International Defense Review*, April 1976, p. 535.
[4] *Jane's Fighting Ships, 1976–77* (New York: McGraw Hill Book Company, 1975), p. 162.
[5] "International Defense Digest," p. 535. For additional details on characteristics, see *Jane's Ships, 1976–77*, p. 719.
[6] "International Defense Digest," p. 535. However, it is possible that the new aircraft may be American-built A-4s. In December 1976 McDonnell Douglas was given government permission to talk with India about possible sales of those planes.
[7] "A Tropical Base for India," *Far Eastern Economic Review*, October 31, 1975, p. 5, and "India: A New Base Off Malaysia," *Defense and Foreign Affairs Daily*, November 3, 1975.
[8] International Institute for Strategic Studies, *The Military Balance 1975–76* (London: Chatto & Windus, 1976), p. 33. Also see the staff report to U.S. Congress, Senate, Subcommittee on Foreign Military Assistance of the Committee on Foreign Relations, *U.S. Military States to Iran*, July 1976, p. 23.
[9] The subject has been broached with the United States and Great Britain, although neither country seems yet willing to provide aircraft carriers to Iran.

Apparently in preparation for expanding their role in the Indian Ocean, the Iranians have been constructing a massive air and naval base at Chah Bahar in southeastern Iran, a location with easy access to that body of water. In addition, it is said that the Iranians have acquired basing rights from Mauritius,[10] and that the Shah has even broached the subject of joint military pacts with countries such as Australia and New Zealand.[11] These actions, together with the procurement of sophisticated, long-range air and naval craft and certain statements by the Shah, indicate that Iran envisages a much broader military role for itself in the Indian Ocean region.

In any discussion of major regional naval powers with a long-range capability, Australia should also be included. As reflected in Table A-3, Australia's fleet could operate many miles from its shores. It is distinguished at present by possessing the only aircraft carrier other than India's belonging to an Indian Ocean state. To bolster its capability, the Australian navy has ordered two more frigates from the United States.[12]

Of the other states in the area, South Africa and Pakistan are already or soon may be improving their long-range capability. South Africa's seven frigates give its navy a considerable range, which will be increased further when construction of six additional frigates is completed. The latter will be similar to the Joao Continho-class frigate, whose range is some 5,900 miles, and they will reportedly be armed with the outstanding Israeli-produced Gabriel surface-to-surface naval missile.[13] Additionally, South Africa has three French-made Daphne-class submarines, which augment its ability to operate far beyond its own waters, and it has two French-produced Agosta-class submarines on order.

Like South Africa, Pakistan maintains three Daphne-class submarines and has reportedly ordered a fourth. Pakistan's version is

[10] Ann Hessing Cahn, "Determinants of the Nuclear Option: The Case of Iran," in Ankar Marwah and Ann Schulz, eds., *Nuclear Proliferation and the Near Nuclear Countries* (Cambridge, Mass.: Ballinger, 1975), p. 197, and Shahram Chubin, "Naval Competition and Security in South-West Asia," in *Power at Sea: III. Competition and Conflict*, Adelphi Paper 124 (London: International Institute for Strategic Studies, 1976), p. 25.

[11] Robert Manning, "Iran's Powerful Empire Builder," *Far Eastern Economic Review*, January 24, 1975, pp. 20-21.

[12] *Jane's Ships, 1976–77*, p. 36. There have been reports, however, of potential financial problems surrounding the purchase of the Perry-class frigates because inflation has added significantly to the original cost of these highly sophisticated ships. Nevertheless, Australia will most likely not be able to terminate the agreement without considerable problems. See Stephen Barber, "Frigate Deal Turns Sour," *Far Eastern Economic Review*, June 25, 1976, p. 13.

[13] *Jane's Ships, 1976–77*, pp. 382, 398.

slightly modified and is generally referred to as a Hangor class. Although the range of this version is not known, it probably has approximately the same 4,500-mile capability at five knots as the French Daphne.[14] In addition, Pakistan has two British-type frigates, and a couple of the more modern Whitby class have been acquired from London.[15]

Indonesia, too, has acquired a sizable navy with a considerable long-range capability, which is not surprising in a country comprising far-flung islands. With twelve frigates, sixteen corvettes, and three active Whiskey-class submarines, Indonesia's navy could probably patrol large swaths of the Indian Ocean. At present, however, it faces maintenance and other difficulties that severely limit its operational strength.

The armies of the littoral states are impressive, both for their huge amounts of weaponry and for the number of men under arms. Indeed, the combined total of men in the regular armies of those countries exceeds 3 million—more than the regular armies of the United States and the Soviet Union put together! Even the addition of the United States Marine Corps does not increase the superpowers' total to 3 million. There are, of course, huge differences between the manpower and the amount and quality of equipment of the armies of the superpowers and those of most Indian Ocean states. Yet for purposes of description, comparing the numbers illustrates how much emphasis the littoral countries place on the military, and the degree to which there may or may not be a palpable power vacuum.

Such a large number of men under arms makes necessary a vast amount of equipment, and, as Table A-5 shows, the littoral states, especially India, Iran, and Pakistan, have amassed a sizable amount of armor. In addition, Iran has on order 1,730 more tanks, of which 1,480 are the excellent British-made Chieftain model.[16] Although Iran enjoys an edge over the other states in the quality of its tanks, both the Indian and the Pakistani forces can count on large numbers of combat-experienced crews.

---

[14] Ibid., p. 165.

[15] Ibid., p. 352.

[16] *Military Balance, 1976–77*, p. 33. It is also interesting to note that 1,200 of the Chieftains will be the newest version with a recently developed type of armor and an improved engine and transmission. The armor has been described by the British secretary of state for defense as representing the most significant breakthrough of the last three decades in tank design as well as in protection. Even before these improvements, the Chieftain was considered the best tank in the world by many armor experts. For additional details, see "Improved Chieftain for Iran," *International Defense Review*, August 1976, p. 640-642.

The large amounts of armor held by the littoral states have naturally created a demand for appropriate defenses. The anti-armor arsenals of these states include American-made TOW, French-produced ENTAC, and SS-11 antitank guided weapons (ATGWs) in Iran; German-produced Cobra ATGWs in Pakistan; and ENTACs and SS-11s in India. Some of the same and similar anti-armor weapons can be found in the inventories of other littoral states. There is also a wide array of air-to-surface missiles on combat aircraft owned by the states.

Any assessment of overall military power in the region must focus on India because it has the greatest number of men under arms and, not surprisingly, the largest quantity of weapons. A significant proportion of its aircraft, ships, armor, and missiles is modern, and, more important, the Indian armed forces have demonstrated their ability to utilize it.

During the 1971 war with Pakistan, Indian naval units sought out and destroyed a sizable portion of Pakistan's navy. Similarly, India's army and air force successfully fought against their Pakistani counterparts and demonstrated a reasonable degree of coordination and support. Since 1971, the Indians appear to have devoted considerable effort to absorbing the military lessons of the conflict. In addition, New Delhi seems to intend not only to maintain its present regional power position but to increase its military strength. Without any question, no other Indian Ocean state could defeat India's armed forces in a conventional war, and even the People's Republic of China would face great difficulties following its probable early successes in the mountainous border areas.

In the wake of its defeat, Pakistan, the traditional foe of India, has resumed military preparations and has shown little willingness to accept Indian hegemony. On the contrary, it appears to be making ready for a possible future conflict with its giant neighbor. If hostilities do erupt in the near future, Pakistan probably cannot defeat India by itself, but it is making distinct progress in rearming and modernizing its military. In any future conflict, it will not face the tremendous disadvantage of trying to defend a part of the country some 1,000 miles away, as in the 1971 war.

In general, both nations have the advantage of large numbers of combat-trained personnel, but in the past they have been dependent upon other countries for the bulk of their armaments. India, however, has made great strides in developing an indigenous weapons industry, which seems to be one of the most extensive in the region.

Elsewhere, Iran has a very modern arsenal and in some areas can boast of the most sophisticated weapons in the region, for example, F-14s and Chieftain tanks. But the Iranians lack sufficient numbers of combat-experienced and technically skilled personnel to utilize all of that equipment efficiently. The thousands of American advisers in the country are now training the Iranians to use the new weapons, and, if Iran should become involved in a war, many of those Americans may operate them, particularly if their failure to do so might endanger them or their families.

As mentioned earlier, the Indonesian navy has found it troublesome just to patrol the scattered parts of that island nation. The air force and army face similar difficulties. Thus, the Indonesian armed forces should be viewed primarily for their future power potential, which is significant. If Indonesia completes its transition from the use of Soviet military equipment and manages to develop a cohesive force with high morale, it could attain a potent defense capability. This seems unlikely before the mid-1980s.

A nation worth noting for its military sophistication is Australia, whose regular units per man appear to be the best equipped and trained in the area. Although the Australian forces are not as great as those of other countries in the region, they are capable of defending the homeland against any nonsuperpower threat. Furthermore, they could probably intercept seaborne threats many miles away, especially in conjunction with other major forces, though the loss of a dozen ASW aircraft in a fire in December 1976 will at least temporarily impair that capability. Apart from the vast extent of the area to be defended, Australia's principal difficulty probably lies in the command and control of its forces. Until recently, Canberra's forces were prepared to face threats jointly with either British or American units and not independently.

On the western side of the ocean lies racially troubled, but militarily powerful, South Africa. Like the Australians, the South Africans boast a modern well-trained military, but their aircraft do not have the same range or striking power. Nonetheless, South Africa maintains the best armed force south of the Sahara.

Farther to the north, the Ethiopians and Somalis are busily engaged in arms competition, and for the moment the latter have the advantage. Unless Somalia can continue to count on large numbers of Cuban, East European, and, particularly, Russian advisers, however, its prospects for absorbing and using these arms are limited. Because of its lack of manpower, Somalia would require active involvement by foreign troops in order to wage a successful war against

Ethiopia in the near future. Indeed, though both states are equipped and trained to defend their borders against each other, neither could carry out any military offensive beyond guerrilla operations without outside assistance.

On the whole, an examination of the armed forces of the countries indigenous to the Indian Ocean region reveals the presence of a huge number of men under arms and large stocks of materiel, hardly reflective of a real power vacuum. As many of the tables at the end of this study reflect, these weapons are often quite sophisticated and, in fact, can be used for military purposes other than mere defense of the homeland. Thus the acquisition of a meaningful nuclear capability by any one of these countries would transform it into a major offensive threat. Also, it is evident that there has been a large increase in the inventories of weapons throughout the region since the announcement of the British intent to withdraw from east of the Suez in 1968.

The explosion on May 18, 1974, of an atomic device by India opened a new chapter in its military potential and has already altered the perceptions of other states in the region. Not surprisingly, Pakistan appears interested in keeping pace with its rival: Prime Minister Bhutto long ago stated his intention of having nuclear weapons.[17] And there has been speculation that in time Iran may decide to abrogate its adherence to the nonproliferation treaty.[18] This eventuality might be more probable if India began to build nuclear weapons.

Iraq, which already has a very small reactor, could eventually become an atomic power, though it would need nearly a decade to build adequate facilities. Other countries, such as South Africa and Australia, could also develop nuclear weapons in the near future, if they decided on that course.

This discussion has covered only those countries most likely to embark on a nuclear-weapons production program. It should also be kept in mind that any littoral nation might procure ready-made atomic weapons from nuclear powers, even though such an event seems unlikely.

Nonsuperpower External Actors in the Indian Ocean

Both Great Britain and France had considerable colonial interests in the Indian Ocean area, especially the British. As the Western

[17] S. S. Ghauri, "Bhutto's Nuclear Plans Opposed," *Far Eastern Economic Review*, July 30, 1976, p. 26.
[18] For a more detailed discussion of Iran's proliferation incentives and disincentives, see Cahn, "Determinants," pp. 194-198.

powers relinquished control over various possessions, they usually sustained their political, economic, and, in many instances, military relations. In recent times, the French and British have vacated facilities in the littoral states even though they could have remained under certain circumstances. The government of Singapore, for example, reportedly preferred that London retain its forces in the country.

The British and French decisions seem to have been based primarily upon economic arguments. Yet both states continue to have important trade and investment interests in the region, and neither has permanently discontinued its military presence there. No matter how much Britain and France have decreased active patrols, they could reverse themselves and even regain the use of some needed facilities.

Not all the actions of the two Western powers have been designed to reduce their military presence in the Indian Ocean. Paris has added to its forces in the area submarines capable of carrying nuclear missiles.[19] This step undoubtedly resulted from France's decision to create a more mobile navy, at least in part because it lost its major base at Diego Suarez in Madagascar. In April 1976, it was reported that France would, for an "indefinite" period of time, "maintain a fleet of some twenty warships in the Indian Ocean."[20] As early as September 1973, France had created an Indian Ocean naval command and, the following spring, augmented its task force with a helicopter carrier. The French navy also operated naval patrol aircraft from Djibouti.[21]

There has been much discussion about the circumstances under which the French will depart Djibouti, such as whether they will retain rights to the facility for any significant period of time and under what contingencies they could use it. Although these questions remain unanswered, it is known that France does not require Djibouti in order to maintain a naval presence in the area, since its principal naval base there is the island of Réunion.[22] Of course, permanent exclusion from Djibouti would necessitate the establishment of a new Red Sea base or the stationing of a carrier in the region for the naval patrol flights to continue. It is important to note that the French gov-

---

[19] John P. Wallach, "Cuban Troops in Somalia," *Baltimore News-American*, March 10, 1976.

[20] Desmond Wettern, "French Keep 20 Ships in Indian Ocean," *London Daily Telegraph*, April 15, 1976.

[21] James Laurie, "The Hardware for Potential Confrontation," *Far Eastern Economic Review*, May 27, 1974, pp. 30-34. This article contains additional information about French and other deployments during that period.

[22] Wettern, "French Keep 20 Ships."

ernment reportedly contends that its Indian Ocean forces "are not really connected with Djibouti." [23]

The British have also preserved their presence, though obviously at a lesser level than in previous years. Until recently they regularly patrolled the ocean with a guided-missile destroyer, five destroyer escorts and support ships, and aircraft.[24] Future deployments of a smaller size are possible, but such patrols would probably be infrequent. Nevertheless, these naval activities emphatically testify to the determination of the British to keep close watch on the Indian Ocean area when it is in their interest.

British plans to deploy a task group of some ten ships east of Suez in early April 1976 were cancelled because of the "cod war" with Iceland.[25] The settlement of that conflict has freed those and additional ships for duty elsewhere. Thus, despite Britain's decrease in military commitments and activities around the world, it still maintains a limited capability to deploy forces to selected regions, such as the Indian Ocean.

It is possible that at least one new external power, the People's Republic of China (PRC), may establish itself militarily in the Indian Ocean. A Chinese presence would probably be directed initially against the U.S.S.R., especially if submarines are sent. Chinese submarines with nuclear-tipped missiles, like similar U.S. vessels, would pose a serious threat to Moscow's heartland if deployed into the northern Indian Ocean. More important in a regional context, the entrance of the PRC would add to the number of states that could become involved in local conflicts and relations between area states. Some Indian writers were already expressing concern over a possible Chinese deployment in the early 1970s.[26]

There is no reason to believe that the PRC could send any sizable force to the region for some years. Reports suggest that it may have encountered difficulties in the design of its ballistic-missile nuclear submarines, which may prevent their completion until early in the next decade or later. However, the Chinese can already produce liquid-fueled rockets.[27] In the conventional mode, Peking's navy is

[23] Ibid.
[24] Center for Defense Information, "The Indian Ocean: A New Naval Arms Race" (Washington, D.C.: Center for Defense Information, April 1974).
[25] Wettern, "French Keep 20 Ships."
[26] See Devendra Kaushik, The Indian Ocean: Towards a Zone of Peace (Delhi: Vikas Publications, 1972), pp. 62-71, and A.P.S. Bindra, "The Indian Ocean as Seen by an Indian," U.S. Naval Institute Proceedings, May 1970.
[27] Jane's Ships, 1976–77, p. 103.

rather large and while somewhat aged, potentially powerful, though with limited capability for distant operations.

A Chinese entanglement in Indian Ocean affairs could stem from their proferred guarantee against Indian "nuclear blackmail," which has obviously pleased Pakistan.[28] This action undoubtedly will continue to rankle India as Chinese surface and naval missile programs advance.

The only other nonsuperpower considered capable of establishing an Indian Ocean presence is Japan, but, given its postwar behavior, the likelihood is remote. Japan has enjoyed considerable economic success over the last several decades without spending a large portion of its budget on defense, and there would seem to be little advantage in beginning to do so at this time. Merely to create a fleet to defend its oil lines to the Persian Gulf would entail a tremendous expense, and a buildup of that magnitude would raise fears among most littoral states. Consequently, Tokyo will probably limit its activities in the Indian Ocean to occasional naval visits to a few states on the eastern periphery, like the goodwill visit by a squadron of four destroyers to Malaysia.[29]

---

[28] Christopher Lewis, ed., *Asia 1975 Yearbook* (Hongkong: Far Eastern Economic Review, 1975), p. 251. Also see *Peking Review*, July 5, 1974, p. 14.

[29] Kaushik, *Indian Ocean*, p. 58.

2

THE SUPERPOWERS AND THE INDIAN OCEAN

Soviet Naval Activity

Over the past decade the Soviet Union has steadily increased the size of its force in the Indian Ocean. The combatants vary in number, though fewer than ten is typical. An unusual number of Soviet ships was deployed in the area in 1971, when Moscow had six surface combatants and six submarines on station. This strength was reached about three weeks after a U.S. task force was sent there apparently as a show of force during the war between India and Pakistan. Moscow's Indian Ocean squadron generally consists of cruisers, destroyers, destroyer escorts, and attack submarines, and in the past has sometimes been augmented by the 18,000-ton helicopter carrier *Leningrad*.[1]

During their visits to the Indian Ocean, Soviet vessels use facilities at a number of places, including Chittagong, Vishakhapatnam, Mogadishu, Madagascar, Mauritius, and anchorages off the Seychelles and Socotra Island. Other key facilities, because of their location on or near two major appendages of the Indian Ocean, are Aden, Hodeida, Berbera, and Umm Qasr. The last is the only Persian Gulf base available to Moscow, and the other three give it access to the Red Sea. Of course, the Soviet Union neither uses these facilities exclusively nor controls them, though it has improved many of them.

What are the reasons for this growing Soviet interest in the Indian Ocean, and what are the implications of this interest? These and other questions are troubling American decision makers, as well they should, and the answers are neither simple nor, in some cases, easy to accept.

---

[1] R. M. Paone, "The Big Three and the Indian Ocean," *Sea Power*, August 1975, p. 28.

First, the Soviet Union is merely acting like the world's second ranking superpower, in keeping with the current balance of power. Since the West has enjoyed significant influence in the region for the last fifty years, and even longer, Moscow is using a tactic it has employed successfully elsewhere: it is attempting to gain a foothold in an area controlled by the West. In so doing, the Soviet Union hopes to take advantage of any Western mistakes or, at a minimum, to prevent the West from exercising unfettered influence in the area.

Some limited military advantages to a presence would accrue to the Russians, including the possibility of disrupting merchant shipping lines in the event of war with the United States and/or the Western powers. But for such an effort to have a telling effect, Moscow would require a much larger force in the region. At any rate, the disruption of merchant shipping would probably not assume crucial proportions in a war between the United States and the Soviet Union because of the likelihood of rapid escalation beyond the conventional mode. In fact, such action in itself could trigger a nuclear exchange, and Moscow has shown reluctance to carry events that far.

In a practical sense, the Soviet presence will therefore carry more weight during periods of peace and will act as a counter to Western military intervention in the area, though that will probably not occur in the wake of the American involvement in Vietnam. Some may argue that Moscow is building a capability to intervene in the littoral states, but it could not possibly do so now. In the past the Soviet Union has normally not risked sending forces into noncontiguous countries and probably would not do so in an Indian Ocean littoral state. Thus, Moscow will probably continue to support liberation forces operating along the littoral and encourage other Communist states to engage in similar efforts.

It could be argued that Moscow has been responding to American naval activity in the area, though it would be difficult to prove how much of its increase can be attributed to actions by Washington. That the Soviet Union does respond to U.S. actions in this way was underscored by former director of the Central Intelligence Agency William Colby when, in response to questions about the building of facilities on Diego Garcia, he indicated that the surge in Soviet deployments into the Indian Ocean has "been highly responsive to U.S. naval activities." [2] Of particular concern to Moscow are the American nuclear ballistic-missile submarines of the Polaris and Poseidon variety and

[2] Hearing before U.S. Congress, Senate, Committee on Armed Services, *Disapprove Construction Projects on the Island of Diego Garcia*, 94th Cong. 1st sess., June 10, 1975, p. 31.

the prospect of eventual deployment of Trident submarines into the region when they become operational within the next several years. The Tridents will carry missiles in the 3,000-4,000-nautical-mile range with multiple independent reentry vehicle warheads, and, if the proposed concept can be implemented, the range of the missile will eventually reach some 6,000 miles. The American strategic missile submarines now available for deployment in the Indian Ocean are generally armed with nuclear missiles in the 1,725- and 2,880-mile ranges.[3]

For the most part, Soviet naval activities seem to be oriented toward keeping a small force in the region that can be enlarged during a crisis. This was done not only in the wake of the Indo-Pakistani war but also in response to the sending of a U.S. carrier task group into the Indian Ocean during the 1973 October conflict in the Middle East. Both instances served as vehicles for Moscow's signaling capability, that is, they made known its intention of not being cowed. Yet, by having no permanent bases and no large permanent naval presence, the U.S.S.R. was able to avoid the political and economic costs generally associated with such a policy.

Since 1975 Moscow has added to its limited military presence by making long-range aerial reconnaissance flights over the Indian Ocean. These flights are similar to those conducted by the United States, though in a somewhat less sophisticated manner.[4]

Kremlin leaders are probably as suspicious of U.S. actions in the Indian Ocean as Americans often are of Russian activities and goals. The U.S.S.R. may fear that U.S. naval units might someday attempt to disrupt Soviet merchant shipping lines, intervene militarily in the affairs of a littoral state, or hinder Soviet efforts to conduct legitimate business in the area, even at the risk of nuclear war.

The Russians already have a number of economic interests in the region and may develop stronger ones. Their trawler fleets, in addition to engaging in intelligence activities, fish extensively in the world's seas. As many fishing grounds become restricted by the declaration of 200-mile economic zones, the Indian Ocean will be even more attractive, especially if the lucrative fishing grounds of the North Sea and off the North and South American continents are partially restricted. The Russians' interest in the Indian Ocean may also be related to the potentially rich fishing grounds near Antarctica.

---

[3] Jane's Ships, 1976–77, pp. 540-544; Jane's Weapon Systems, 1976 (New York: McGraw-Hill Book Company, 1975), pp. 180-182. The range of the first Tridents to be deployed will probably be only some 3,000-4,000 miles.

[4] For a detailed comparison of the various naval reconnaissance aircraft of the two superpowers, see Jane's All the World's Aircraft, 1975–76 (New York: McGraw-Hill Book Company, 1975).

Chronic difficulties in producing sufficient food supplies have been an Achilles' heel to the U.S.S.R. and have subjected Moscow to pressures from its primary competitors in the international arena. The Russian leaders are particularly sensitive to what they consider inappropriate American efforts to tie trade between the two countries to internal changes within the Soviet Union. In view of these difficulties, the Soviet Union could hardly fail to aspire to harvesting as much as possible from the Indian Ocean.

The Soviet Union may also have designs on oil or other minerals thought to underlie parts of the Indian Ocean. It may reason that without some presence in the area, it would not get an equal opportunity to exploit those valuable resources. Closer to shore, it may want to compete with the United States for offshore concessions from the littoral states. Although they could derive political advantages from such concessions, the Russians may have another aim. In view of the extensive resources located in its own great land mass, the U.S.S.R. may be interested less in exploiting the mineral and fossil fuel wealth than in denying it to the Western alliance. Of course, these objectives are not mutually exclusive, and the Kremlin leadership would probably prefer to accomplish both, since all natural resources are finite. If resources are available at a reasonable cost elsewhere, the Soviet ruling elite may want to save its own finite minerals and fossil fuels. Certainly such long-term reasoning would not be unusual for a superpower that intends to remain competitive with, or even surpass, the other major powers during the coming century.

The Soviet presence in the Indian Ocean may reflect an effort to prepare for the advent of Chinese naval units or submarines with ballistic missiles aimed at the Soviet Union. Short of that, the Kremlin may be girding itself for intensified competition with Peking, which has been active in some littoral states in eastern Africa and the southern tip of the Arabian peninsula and in Pakistan. The Chinese ventures have been comparatively small, and Peking will not pose a serious regional challenge to Moscow in the near future.

The Soviet Union may suspect that some littoral states might seize Russian vessels, particularly fishing trawlers, at some future date, if those nations forbid Soviet boats from their claimed waters. Such concerns would probably prompt it to protect its economic interests. The Kremlin's own intentions in regard to the 200-mile economic resources zone, if completely known, might illuminate its motives.

Any consideration of Soviet military activity in the Indian Ocean must weigh the possibility that it is aimed at injuring the interests of the United States. But there is little evidence that the Kremlin is planning military action against either the American forces or any of the area states. Moscow has generally reacted to U.S. naval activity in the area and has scrupulously avoided confrontations that could ignite a nuclear war. Although Moscow's efforts are not in consonance with Washington's interests in the region, the U.S.S.R. has attempted to maintain competition between the two superpowers at a peaceful level.

In general, the Kremlin seems to have learned what Great Britain, the United States, and other great powers throughout history have known—that building a powerful navy, while costly, can earn significant economic and political rewards in addition to military ones. Moscow also recognizes the navy's deterrent strength: in a 1970 Navy Day speech Admiral Sergei Gorshkov said, "the presence of our ships . . . ties the imperialists' hands and deprives them of the opportunity freely to interfere in the people's internal affairs." [5]

On the other hand, Moscow doubtlessly understands that there are limitations to such power as well as to the amount of resources available to expend on it. Consequently, it is entirely possible that the Russian leaders may prefer not to build a sizable naval fleet for deployment to the Indian Ocean, particularly if they are convinced that their chief rival, though willing to deploy naval units to the area, would restrain itself if the Soviet Union does the same. A massive effort in the Indian Ocean would compel Russian leaders either to decrease the quality and strength of their other fleets (thus far combatants stationed in the region have been diverted from the northern and western forces) or allocate their limited resources to the construction of an independent fleet. In other words, Moscow probably faces a situation familiar to Washington: hard decisions are required to apportion the available resources among the various parts of the defense budget. In sum, these considerations suggest that the Soviet leaders might prefer not to build a sizable navy for deployment to the Indian Ocean, particularly if they believed that the United States would exercise similar restraint in the area.

American Naval Activity

The United States has maintained an impressive naval presence in the Indian Ocean with carrier task forces and all their accoutrements, including seventy to eighty aircraft on the *Hancock* class, some eighty-

---

[5] Admiral Sergei C. Gorshkov, translated and published under the title *Red Star Rising at Sea* (Annapolis: United States Naval Institute, 1974).

five planes on the *Kitty Hawk*, and up to ninety-five on the *Enterprise*. Each carrier task force is usually accompanied by five or six destroyers and destroyer escorts and a nuclear attack submarine. When such a force is in the region, it is generally agreed that the U.S. units have a significant naval advantage over their Soviet counterparts. In late January 1977, an all-nuclear powered U.S. carrier task force was dispatched to the Indian Ocean for the first time in twelve years, an action described by the U.S. Navy as a "routine deployment."

In the absence of a carrier force, the augmented American presence usually consists of a task force headed by a guided-missile cruiser, escorted by destroyers and often by attack submarines. When neither carrier nor cruiser-headed task forces are stationed in the Indian Ocean, responsibility for the area falls on the American Middle East Force, which operates from Bahrain. The Middle East Force, comprising a command ship and two destroyers, deploys into the Arabian Sea and occasionally the Red Sea, in addition to the Persian Gulf. Washington has undoubtedly worried Moscow by deploying ballistic missile-firing submarines in the northern Indian Ocean–Arabian Sea area. These deployments have made the Soviet Union ever more vulnerable to U.S. nuclear weapons, and the advent of Trident submarines will heighten that vulnerability. Of course, there are also deployments of other U.S. submarines of the attack variety, which do not carry nuclear weapons.

Why does the United States maintain such an extensive naval presence in the Indian Ocean? What are U.S. interests in the area? Does Moscow pose a significant threat to Washington's interests? Is it advisable to expand Diego Garcia? These questions must be answered in order to arrive at an understanding of U.S. naval activities in the Indian Ocean and their major ramifications.

A frequently heard justification for the U.S. presence is that the British withdrawal from east of Suez left a power vacuum, which the Soviet Union has attempted to fill. After Moscow sent naval forces into the region, some observers felt that it was trying to exert political pressure on various littoral states and that an American counterbalance was called for.

Other arguments posit the notion that Soviet activity in the area stems from the historic Russian desire to obtain a warm-water port or an overland route through littoral countries bordering the Soviet Union. The latter could be won only if the naval pressure were sufficient to intimidate neighboring governments into yielding such access.

In recent years, the argument most often heard has been that the Russians are positioning their naval forces to enable them to interfere with the shipment of oil from the Persian Gulf. This capability would subject the western European allies to the mercy of the Soviet Union because most of those countries depend on Persian Gulf petroleum for their industries and homes and, in some cases, nearly their entire economies. The same vulnerability threatens America's most important East Asian ally, Japan. Therefore, this argument contends, the United States simply cannot afford to allow the Soviet Union to have the most powerful fleet in the area.

It is sometimes said that, at the least, the Russians may gain enough political leverage among the littoral states to make it difficult for the United States to deal with the oil-producing countries and that, at most, the U.S.S.R. could actually prevent the shipment of petroleum by military means. Of course, the Soviet Union would probably never resort to this military option unless it believed that the United States would give up this key resource without using nuclear weapons.

It has also been contended that deployment of Western navies into the Indian Ocean has been positively (though tacitly) accepted by most of the littoral states, but the increase in greater Soviet naval activity poses a threat to this accommodation. If there is not a corresponding increase in the U.S. naval force, many of those states will lose their resolve to resist Soviet influence.

The arguments outlined thus far have focused on the negative side of U.S. interests in the region, specifically the need to develop a greater naval presence because of Soviet activity. On the positive side, access to the region's resources, especially oil, is of prime concern, not only to the United States but also to its Western European allies and Japan. Also, there are legitimate private American investments in the littoral countries, which should not be endangered by social, economic, and political change there. In this connection, the United States can be expected to make every effort to thwart the economic and political advance of the Soviet Union, and especially to prevent the takeover of any littoral state by a Communist regime friendly to Moscow. The American government would also be likely to oppose any offer by a littoral state of facilities to visiting Soviet naval units.

Such a challenge may confront the United States in southern Africa. While it is certainly not in the American interest to support the white minority-ruled governments in Pretoria and Salisbury, despite their anti-Communist policies, it is also not in the American interest to allow a Communist or Moscow-oriented regime to gain power in Rhodesia or South Africa. The matter is complicated by a

21

variety of economic, political, and military reasons for maintaining good relations with any government in the two countries.

Although it is not essential for the United States or its allies to utilize South Africa's military facilities, the Western position in the area would be weakened if, for example, the Soviet Union were to gain access to the excellent naval facilities at Simonstown. If Moscow were also to find friendly regimes along the East African littoral, its capabilities in the western Indian Ocean would certainly be enhanced. Thus, in South Africa, the United States has both a positive interest, in obtaining its raw materials, and a negative interest, in preventing its resources and military facilities from falling under Soviet hegemony.

Another aspect of the American presence in the Indian Ocean that cannot be overlooked centers on Diego Garcia, a coral atoll located in the Chagos Archipelago, about a thousand miles south of India in the north central Indian Ocean. The largest of fifty-two islands in the chain, Diego Garcia was first discovered by a Portuguese of that name in 1532. In the eighteenth century some French colonists settled there, but during the Napoleonic Wars, the British seized the island.

In 1966, Britain and the United States concluded a fifty-year agreement calling for joint construction of a military communications facility on Diego Garcia. The United States has been responsible for all major activity on the island ever since, and in the first five years constructed roads, fuel depots, a runway for large transports, and a facility to improve communications with American nuclear submarines.

Afterward, the question of how much the United States should utilize Diego Garcia became a matter of considerable controversy, both in the United States and among the littoral states. In July 1975, Congress, by a close vote in the Senate, empowered the navy to build a base and support facility on the island. As a result, the runway is being increased in length from 8,000 feet to 12,000 feet so that larger aircraft, including B-52 strategic bombers and KC-135 tanker aircraft, can use Diego Garcia.[6] Fuel storage capacities for aviation will be increased from 60,000 barrels to 380,000 barrels, and 320,000 barrels of fuel oil will be available for ships.[7] The total storage capacity should eventually provide enough fuel to supply the needs

---

[6] According to former Defense Secretary James Schlesinger, the runways would require considerable strengthening to handle loaded B-52s. See Senate Committee on Armed Services, *Disapprove Construction*, p. 39. Little has been said, however, about the lighter B-1.

[7] See June 10, 1975, press briefing by then Secretary of Defense James Schlesinger.

of a typical carrier task force for twenty-eight days.[8] The plan calls for the dredging of an anchorage to accommodate a carrier task force and the construction of a pier to provide some 550 feet of berthing, primarily for the rapid loading and unloading of fuel. Also being added are other airfield improvements and power, storage, and ancillary facilities.[9]

A domestic controversy revolved around the possible implications of the Diego Garcia buildup. Senator Mike Mansfield and others saw it as the beginning of a three-ocean navy, with costs as high as $8 billion to construct a third fleet and up to $800 million annually to maintain it. Senate Armed Services Committee Chairman John C. Stennis was among those who supported the Diego Garcia request on the grounds that there was no intention to build a three-ocean navy and that the Defense Department request for a dependable refueling station was reasonable. Senator John Culver retorted that the United States already had refueling rights at thirty-six ports on the Indian Ocean littoral.[10]

According to retired Admiral Elmo R. Zumwalt, Jr., writing about the Defense Department's position, navy professionals brought former Defense Secretary James Schlesinger around to the position of "want[ing] badly to keep a carrier there in the Indian Ocean permanently, which was a clear impossibility because of the strain it would put on the rest of the fleet. . . ." Schlesinger's solution to the problem, according to Zumwalt, was to arrange that the aircraft carriers *Hancock* and *Oriskany*, both of which were to be retired immediately, "should be kept on for another two years until the Diego Garcia issue had been resolved and *Eisenhower*, the third nuclear carrier, was nearer completion."[11]

President Ford, in an effort to persuade critics that the construction on Diego Garcia would not lead to a dangerous and costly naval race with the Soviet Union in the Indian Ocean, stated that "the installation would not imply an increase in the level of U.S. forces deployed to that region."[12] Nevertheless, many people, including Senators Mansfield, Culver, and Stuart Symington, remained unconvinced. When Congress failed to disapprove the President's request, however, work was begun on Diego Garcia.

---

[8] Spencer Rich, "Hill Approves U.S. Base on Diego Garcia," *Washington Post,* July 29, 1975.

[9] Schlesinger press briefing, June 10, 1975.

[10] Rich, "Hill Approves U.S. Base."

[11] Elmo R. Zumwalt, Jr., *On Watch* (New York: Quadrangle, 1976), p. 455.

[12] Rich, "Hill Approves U.S. Base."

An outline of the evolution of American military interest in the island may contribute to an understanding of the controversy surrounding Diego Garcia among the littoral states. Early in the 1960s, long before the British announced their intention to withdraw from east of Suez, the Navy Department expressed interest in converting Diego Garcia into a major facility. It was already predicted that the Soviet Union would establish a naval presence in the region, and U.S. preparations to protect and assist any Polaris submarines there seemed necessary.

When the Russian presence materialized in 1968, the navy renewed these pleas, but the commitment in Vietnam diverted its resources to that conflict. As the navy continued to press for the deployment of American ships into the Indian Ocean to counter Moscow's activities, U.S. carrier task forces were sent there. The Soviet Union responded by increasing the number of its combatants and support ships in the region. Thus the navy's prediction of the development of an ever larger Soviet force was ironically borne out.

Few would argue that even an immensely greater Western deployment would have discouraged a Russian presence, and some question remains whether the strengthening of Western forces might actually have encouraged Moscow to deploy more units and work so diligently to acquire the use of facilities from some littoral states. The largest numbers of Soviet ships seem to have been in the Indian Ocean after the arrival of U.S. carrier forces. Also, Soviet apprehension about the deployment of Polaris, and later Polaris-Poseidon, submarines has undoubtedly spurred the introduction of an anti-submarine warfare capability in the region. Politically, the U.S.S.R. has earned undeniable dividends from U.S. actions: at least partly because of the high visibility of U.S. carrier task forces and the Diego Garcia base, the U.S.S.R. has been able to draw support from some littoral states.

It appears that many of the developing states along the littoral, most of whom have only recently received their independence, resent the establishment of military bases by either of the superpowers. Their leaders often perceive such actions as a neocolonialist attempt to gain influence over the internal affairs of the region's nations. Even though it would be difficult to demonstrate that Washington harbors such designs, the charge has credibility to the emerging nations, particularly when their leaders and citizens realize that the United States is building the only Indian Ocean military base to be controlled by a superpower.

The Soviet Union has gained a political advantage among the littoral states by supporting the concept that the Indian Ocean should be a nuclear-free zone of peace, which would preclude the establishment of military bases by all nonindigenous powers. Until recently, even pro-American countries like Australia opposed the construction of the Diego Garcia base, on the grounds that it might provoke increased Soviet naval activity. Some of those states have now dropped their objections, and Australia has actually supported the construction publicly. Other states, such as Indonesia, have reasoned that as long as the Soviet Union maintains a military presence, the United States should also be allowed in the area, even if it must build a base. Thus, if the U.S. deployment of carrier task forces prompted increases in the Soviet presence, the Russian reaction—with no less irony—apparently intimidated some traditional U.S. allies into supporting the buildup on Diego Garcia, contributing to the success of the navy's effort.

3

CONFLICT SCENARIOS

As indicated earlier, a massive amount of modern military equipment either already is or soon will be in the hands of the littoral states, which will have a capability of settling disputes, if diplomatic means fail, on a scale far larger than the traditional border skirmishes. As is well known, the possession of large amounts of military hardware by potential belligerents does not necessarily encourage the peaceful resolution of conflicts. Even more sobering is the consideration that any conflict in the Indian Ocean region which erupts into open warfare could ultimately involve the superpowers.

Curiously enough, many of the potential conflicts in themselves would seem of little consequence to the two superpowers. Yet, when a littoral state solicits the support of either superpower against an area state, a buildup by both the United States and the Soviet Union is virtually certain. And the more military units that Washington and Moscow send to the Indian Ocean, the greater the chances for superpower involvement in minor conflicts and for catastrophic miscalculations.

One potential source of conflict for every Indian Ocean littoral state will lie in its attempts to protect its economic rights up to the proposed 200-mile economic resources zones. Even without such extensive limits, conflicts could result from attempts to guard coastal resources against foreign exploitation or ruination as a result of pollution caused by transiting vessels. The interest shown by many littoral states in acquiring small, fast patrol boats armed with missiles and/or rapid-fire, large-caliber guns indicates their concern.

Of course, this concern is not peculiar to the Indian Ocean, but is shared by most of the world's littoral countries. The seizure of American fishing boats by the Peruvian navy demonstrated that the noncombatant ships of a superpower can be halted and fined without provoking a gunboat reaction. The "cod war" between Iceland and Great Britain showed that offshore resources (in that case codfish) are often so prized that traditional friends and allies will risk war over them.

There are two types of conflict that could break out in the Indian Ocean offshore areas, particularly if the 200-mile economic resources zone is claimed by a large number of littoral states. The first would involve the ships of the major powers as they extend their search for better fishing grounds and new sources of mineral wealth and fossil fuels. The second would involve disputes between neighboring states over demarcation lines, particularly in regard to small uninhabited islands or rocks. Such problems have occurred even before the 200-mile economic resources zones were claimed.

Having touched upon the most important potential source of conflict in the region, this discussion will now focus on specific local problems of the littoral states that could bring about external interference.

East Africa and the Persian Gulf

On the East African littoral, a race war in southern Africa provides one of the most plausible war scenarios among Indian Ocean littoral countries. The white minority rule in South Africa and Rhodesia has given rise not only to indigenous black opposition forces in both countries but also to liberation forces in neighboring lands. The recent civil war in Angola fostered considerable speculation about possible national liberation struggles in South West Africa (Namibia) and South Africa, while the victory of liberation forces in Mozambique increased the possibility of a similar spread from that front.

The situation in Rhodesia, whose population of some 6,273,000 includes only about 270,000 whites, is ripe for violence. The weakness of the white government's position and its inability to turn the black nationalist tide manifests itself in several ways. First, neighboring countries that harbor members of the black liberation movements would make Rhodesia easy prey to externally assisted insurgency. Second, lacking a powerful economy, Rhodesia has been unable to offer sufficient incentives to deter Mozambique, for example, from closing its border. Third, Rhodesia is weak militarily and depends almost entirely on other countries (especially South Africa) for supplies. The ultimate day of reckoning may only await the moment the black nationalist factions can reconcile their differences and unite.

The guerrilla activity in Rhodesia testifies to the likelihood of a violent solution to the racial conflict, but the black nationalist movement has been hindered by the factional struggle. One group, the Zimbabwe African People's Union (ZAPU), led by Joshua Nkomo, has traditionally been supported by the Soviet Union. Considered the most moderate of the black nationalists, Nkomo agreed to hold constitutional talks with Prime Minister Ian Smith to work out a peaceful transition to majority rule. Another faction, the Reverend Ndabaningi Sithole's Zimbabwe African National Union (ZANU), has been aided by the Chinese and more recently the Soviet Union. Two other groups, the Front for the Liberation of Zimbabwe (Frolzi) and Bishop Abel Muzorewa's African National Council (ANC), attempted to unite the movement by joining ZAPU and ZANU in the formation of a new ANC. A rift between Nkomo on one side and Muzorewa and Sithole on the other, however, renewed the internecine struggle, which led Sithole to found the Zimbabwe Liberation Council (ZLC).

The collapse of the Nkomo-Smith talks in March 1976 exacerbated an already tense situation. In the black-white struggle, the breakdown was ushered in by these events: guerrilla activity was extended to the full length of the 800-mile border with Mozambique; Mozambique closed the border; Zambia declared a state of emergency in anticipation of war in Rhodesia and announced that it would work with Mozambique in an effort to attain justice in Rhodesia; and the Soviet Union augmented arms shipments to guerrillas based in Mozambique. In the intrablack power struggle, the failure of the negotiations prompted denunciations of Nkomo, calls for his resignation, and avowals by various factions of recourse to warfare as the only solution, as the prospect of an Angola-style civil war loomed larger.

Under these circumstances, a war scenario in Rhodesia might include invasions by guerrillas from both Mozambique and Zambia, possibly aided by Cuban troops as in Angola. These invasions could well be launched by different factions, and they could culminate in further civil war among the liberation forces. Whether white Rhodesia's only possibly ally, South Africa, would render it assistance is subject to question. The South African government appears reluctant to support what it considers a virtual lost cause, as was illustrated by its efforts to influence Rhodesia to come to terms with the black nationalists.

War is less likely to erupt in South Africa than in Rhodesia. In contrast to its neighbor, South Africa has built the largest military arsenal in Africa south of the Sahara and a domestic economy equipped to sustain it. Also in contrast to Rhodesia, South Africa can exert economic leverage on its neighbors. It conducts enough business with Botswana, for example, to dissuade it from closing their common frontier. Also in contrast to the Rhodesian government, which has relied on the internecine divisions among the blacks for its survival, South Africa has taken command of domestic opposition by legally prohibiting dissident organizations and instituting an effective network of police informers.

The principal South African black liberation groups, the African National Congress (ANC) and the Pan-Africanist Congress (PAC), have been forced to operate mainly in exile. As a result, the indigenous political consciousness required to overthrow such a well-protected regime remains undeveloped and is denied necessary nourishment. The ANC and PAC, however, have been active in neighboring countries and by 1971 had sent hundreds of refugee volunteers to the Soviet bloc and other African countries for military training.[1]

South Africa does not share Rhodesia's problem of being virtually surrounded by countries actively aiding the guerrillas. But the insulation afforded it on one front by its control of South West Africa is deteriorating. The South West African Peoples Organization (SWAPO) is engaging in guerrilla activity with the support of Angola's new regime and is cooperating with the exiled ANC.

Yet no serious threat to South Africa's security is likely until it borders countries actively committed to liberating the South African black population. The South African ANC and PAC may be cooperating with the Rhodesian ZAPU in guerrilla operations against the Rhodesian regime partly in order to create a secure base for operations across the frontier into South Africa.

Northward on the East African littoral in the horn area, critical problems may spring from the concept of Pan-Somalism, a dominant element of Somali foreign policy.[2] This policy seeks to unite under one flag all Somalis, including those living in neighboring countries who were separated from Somalia when Britain, Italy, and Ethiopia drew new borders between 1897 and 1925. These ethnic Somalis in-

---

[1] Irving Kaplan, et al., *Area Handbook for the Republic of South Africa* (Washington, D.C.: American University, 1971), pp. 28-29. This book is a good source for additional historical details. For additional information with a more contemporary emphasis see Tom J. Farer, *War Clouds on the Horn of Africa: A Crisis for Détente* (Washington, D.C.: Carnegie Endowment, 1976).

[2] For a more extensive background on the Somali and Kenyan situation see Irving Kaplan, et al., *Area Handbook for Somalia* (Washington, D.C.: American University, 1969), pp. 224-232, which has been particularly helpful in providing historical details.

habit the Northern Frontier District of Kenya, the Ogaden and Haud regions of southeastern Ethiopia, and the French Territory of the Afars and Issas. Arguing that these frontier demarcations are unjust, the Somali government has publicly manifested concern for the welfare of the neighboring Somalis. It has sought rectification by demanding that they be given the right of self-determination, which it expects them to exercise in favor of joining the Somali Republic.

The Somali constitution states in its introduction that "the Somali Republic promotes, by legal and peaceful means, the union of the Somali territories." [3] The government grants citizenship to all ethnic Somalis, regardless of their country of birth or residence, and the size of the National Assembly remains unlimited to allow for the inclusion of representatives from newly acquired territories. Even the design of the national flag promotes Pan-Somali ambitions: the points of its star represent the five Somali lands to be united, basically the present state and the four areas where ethnic Somalis now reside.[4]

Since neither Kenya nor Ethiopia recognizes the Somali position as reasonable, there will probably be some sort of hostilities. Indeed, since gaining their independence in 1960, the Somalis have engaged in skirmishes with both of their two main neighbors.

At present, the situation involving the Ethiopian regions of Ogaden and Haud and part of the French Territory of the Afars and Issas is the more explosive. The Somalis hold that the preindependence treaties between Britain, Ethiopia, and Italy were not conducted in accordance with previous agreements between the colonial powers and the local Somali tribes. They further claim that, since these tribes were not consulted, the current territorial divisions are illegitimate.

The disputed territories have historically served as seasonal grazing lands for nomadic Somali herdsmen. As early as the first year of Somali independence, the disagreement over these lands provoked border clashes, which escalated into armed conflict between Somalia and Ethiopia in 1964. Although a peace was arranged by the Sudan and the Organization of African Unity, verbal hostility has continued and the potential for further conflict remains.

The spark that could ignite these smoldering issues may emanate from the French Territory of the Afars and Issas. This territory, a part of France with representation in the National Assembly in Paris, is approaching full independence. Somalia fears that more of its ethnics—particularly the Issas—stand in danger of coming under

---

[3] Ibid., p. 226.

[4] Ibid., and James Buxton, "Trouble Brewing in the Horn of Africa," *The Financial Times* (London), June 16, 1976.

Ethiopian rule after years of French and Afar hegemony. At the same time, the Ethiopians are worried that the Somalis may deny them unimpeded access to the territory's main resource, the strategic port of Djibouti. The Franco-Ethiopian railroad runs from there to Addis Ababa, the capital and main city of Ethiopia, and carries some 80 percent of Ethiopian imports and exports. Ethiopia depends more and more on this outlet because the protracted secessionist war in Eritrea has made the other two Ethiopian ports, Assab and Massawa, less accessible.[5] Thus, the mere threat of the loss of Djibouti could compel the Ethiopians to resort to war.

While Ethiopia has signed a formal declaration pledging to respect the integrity and independence of the French Territory, Somalia has declared that this territory must become independent under conditions that give full rights to ethnic Somalis.[6] If these conditions are not fulfilled, Somalia threatens to claim the land. Should it win Djibouti, Somalia would have a lever for exerting pressure on Ethiopia to reduce its control over the other disputed regions.

Since France's announcement at the beginning of 1976 of its intention to release the territory, rival liberation groups have formed, and Afars and Issas have clashed in Djibouti. The Afar president of the Council of Ministers has resigned, and Ethiopian army units have carried out maneuvers in the tri-border area. Meanwhile, Somalia has reportedly moved heavy weaponry north to the same general vicinity and dispatched some 2,000 armed irregulars into Ethiopia's Ogaden.[7]

The United States and the U.S.S.R. have aggravated the situation by giving military assistance to Ethiopia and Somalia, respectively. The United States has maintained a communications facility at Asmara, Ethiopia, and the Soviet Union uses facilities at Berbera, Somalia. Thus, the great powers are juxtaposed through their client states. While the U.S.S.R. appears to be actively supporting Somali ambitions, U.S. backing of Ethiopia seems less firm and irrevocable. Still, a Soviet-sponsored Somali challenge could place the United States in a predicament. Partly at stake, in addition to the territory itself, is strategic control of the Strait of Bab el Mandeb at the entrance to the Red Sea. Somali acquisition of Djibouti therefore holds the promise of strategic gains for the Soviet Union, if it attains a position of influence with Somalia.

---

[5] Michael T. Kaufman, "Tension Increases in French Colony," *New York Times*, July 1, 1976.

[6] Buxton, "Trouble Brewing."

[7] David B. Ottaway, "Ethiopia, Somalia in War Mood," *Washington Post*, July 1, 1976.

The conclusion of the Ethiopia-Somalia conflict probably rests on several variables, the foremost being the presence, if any, that France intends to keep in Djibouti. Continuation of the use of Djibouti as a major base appears unlikely because of the volatility of the situation there: the kidnapping of a busload of French schoolchildren in February 1976 by Somali-based guerrillas underscored this threat in an intensely personal way.[8] France evidently wants to maintain a military presence in the Indian Ocean, but control over the entrance to the Red Sea is not essential. Furthermore, France prefers Réunion and the island of Mayotte in the Comoros as bases. It has intimated that it may leave a small peace-keeping force in Djibouti after independence if the local authorities so desire, but Somalia strongly opposes the idea.[9]

The Soviet Union may discourage the Somalis from directly participating in a takeover of Djibouti in order to avoid antagonizing the Ethiopians, whose new regime has ideological affinities with the U.S.S.R. In that case, the Somalis might either act on their own or try to gain proxy control by relying on the Issas. Of course, there is always the strong likelihood that for a combination of reasons, such as a fear of actual war or a lack of military power, the Somalis may just continue their verbal attacks and their support of the separatist factions.

Another area where Pan-Somalism has flourished is the Northern Frontier District (NFD) of Kenya, which was the southern half of the Jubaland province of Britain's Kenya Colony (the northern part was ceded to Italy in 1925). The British colonial administration, in addition to establishing a colony border, further separated the NFD Somalis by forbidding them from traveling beyond an internal boundary line, in order to suppress intertribal warfare. The Somalis were also taxed at a higher rate than other Africans in Kenya, and they received less economic development aid. These discriminations, which lasted until Kenyan independence in 1963, reinforced the NFD Somalis' sense of identity and solidarity with their northeastern brethren.

During the Kenyan independence talks with the British in 1961, demands by Kenyan Somalis for the separation of their district from Kenya prior to independence prompted an investigation by the colonial administration. The British found an almost unanimous sentiment for independence from Kenya in the NFD, accompanied by diplo-

---

8 James F. Clarity, "French Fly Troops to Djibouti as Somali Rift Widens," *New York Times*, February 6, 1976.

9 Buxton, "Trouble Brewing."

matic pressure from Somalia. They decided not to effect the separation, however, apparently because Kenya was simultaneously being threatened with disintegration by other tribal independence movements. Instead, the colonial administration chose to honor the desires of Kenya's two main political parties, which opposed any dismemberment of their fragile country. To preserve Kenyan unity while possibly trying to appease the Somali minority, the North East Region was created as a federal unit.

These developments solved nothing and resulted only in increasing hostility between Kenya and Somalia, which reached a high point during the so-called Shifta War of 1963–1967. (*Shifta* was the Kenyan term for the Somali guerrilla of the NFD.) Supplied mostly with Soviet and Chinese arms, the Shifta fought the Kenyan police and army and were urged on by the Voice of Somalia.

There has been a period of relative calm since that conflict, but the problem persists. There is little indication of what might rekindle the conflict, but a seemingly unrelated issue could have that effect. For example, relations between Uganda and Kenya became tense after Israelis used bases in Kenya to rescue hijacked hostages at Entebbe, Uganda, in 1976. Uganda, which also has substantial territorial claims on Kenya, sent a military delegation to Somalia, presumably to confer on matters of common interest. If the Ugandan-Kenyan tension had escalated into war, the Somalis would have had a pretext for entering the fray.

Another possible conflict area, the Strait of Bab el Mandeb at the mouth of the Red Sea, could figure prominently not only in the Somali, Ethiopian, and Yemeni (see below) situations but also in any future Arab-Israeli fighting. As Israel and the Arab states step up their preparations for naval warfare, Bab el Mandeb seems ever more likely to become a combat zone, which might involve some of the nearby littoral states.[10]

In South Yemen, the revolutionary regime has been attempting to export revolution to the more conservative states in the region, including Oman, where it has supported the Dhofar rebellion. South Yemen has also had hostile relations with other contiguous states, resulting in border wars with Saudi Arabia in December 1970 and North Yemen in September 1972.

In order to moderate this activity, Saudi Arabia has tried to change South Yemen's political face through infusions of petrodollars.

---

[10] For an extensive treatment of the military forces likely to be involved in any such conflict, see Robert J. Pranger and Dale R. Tahtinen, *Implications of the 1976 Arab-Israeli Military Status* (Washington, D.C.: American Enterprise Institute, 1976).

Taking another tack, North Yemen has been seeking Western arms to augment its defenses and free itself from its former dependency on Soviet weapons. Saudi Arabia has considered funding the arms in the hope of preventing a renewal of Soviet influence over North Yemen and its strategic position on the Strait of Bab el Mandeb.[11] Even though some progress seems to have been made in reducing tensions, the possibility of armed conflict still haunts this critical area.

Among the Persian Gulf countries, a number of foreseeable situations could result in an outbreak of hostilities. Many involve Iran, whose defense preparations seem to be more anticipatory of military conflict than those of any other regional state. The Shah has already taken action in Oman, where he suspects that an unfriendly regime might block the passage of ships, particularly oil tankers, through the critical Straits of Hormuz.[12] By sending troops and additional weapons into Oman in an effort to quell the Dhofar insurgency, the Shah also set a precedent for Iranian intervention on the Arab side of the gulf.

Iran has engaged in some territorial disputes that could erupt again and lead to conflict. In late 1971, a day before the expiration of the British commitment to protect the territorial integrity of the Trucial States, Iran occupied the island of Abu Musa and the Tunbs Islands in the Straits of Hormuz, causing alarm among the Arab states. Iraq ultimately severed diplomatic relations with Iran and with Britain, which it believed to be in collusion with Iran. Since then Iran has concluded agreements with the states of Sharjah, to which Abu Musa belongs, and Ras al Kaymah, of which the Tunbs are a part, but the agreements are not necessarily permanent and frictions could develop, especially in the context of Arab suspicions about Iranian expansionism.

Although the Shah renounced any claim to Bahrain in 1970, Iran might reassert that claim. Such a policy change might be justified on the basis of either the assumption of power by an unfriendly government or the need to protect Bahrain's Iranian minorities.[13] A like situation exists in other gulf sheikhdoms, which have reportedly been pressured to allow greater immigration of Iranians.

---

11 Jack Anderson, "Shift in the Arab World," *Washington Post*, May 2, 1976.
12 For example, see Arnaud de Borchgrave, "Colossus of the Oil Lanes," *Newsweek*, May 21, 1973, p. 40.
13 Enver Koury, *Oil and Geopolitics in the Persian Gulf Area* (Hyattsville, Md.: Institute for North African and Middle Eastern Studies, Inc., 1974), pp. 45-47; Dale R. Tahtinen, *Arms in the Persian Gulf* (Washington, D.C.: American Enterprise Institute, 1974), p. 20.

It should be noted that any Iranian action against a smaller Arab state could provoke a united military response by the Arab world in general, a fact that cannot have escaped the Shah's attention. He also probably realizes that, thanks to the willingness of the United States to sell large amounts of highly sophisticated conventional weapons to his country, Iran is stronger militarily than all of the other gulf countries combined. Nevertheless, it would seem foolhardy for Iran to launch military action against its neighbors without the support of at least one of the superpowers.

Until recently Iran also contended with Iraq over the Shatt-al-Arab River, which marks more than fifty miles of the border between them. The 1975 agreement to end the dispute apparently committed Iran to terminate assistance to the insurgent Kurds in Iraq in exchange for Iraqi concessions on the border.[14]

In general, conflicts could arise from declarations of territorial limits for oil beneath the gulf. Reports several years ago that Iran was considering claiming a fifty-mile territorial limit did little to discourage the common Arab suspicions about Iranian expansionist tendencies.[15] Recent rumors that Iran's oil production has peaked could feed suspicions that Iran may seize minimally defended areas with significant oil reserves.

The historical animosity between the Arab states and non-Arab Iran underlies all of these potential conflicts. Not surprisingly, its basis is largely religious because of the Shah's position as protector of the Shi'ite Moslems, who are generally in competition with the Sunni Moslems. The latter constitute the vast majority in the Arab world with the exception of Iraq, where there is no appreciable difference in numbers between the two sects.

Elsewhere in the gulf, territorial disputes could conceivably flare up. Iraq may decide to reassert its claim to Kuwait, although military action would probably stimulate a response from Iran, Saudi Arabia, or even Syria. As with Iran, provocation of that magnitude would be both risky and unlikely without a commitment of superpower support.

Farther to the southeast, Saudi Arabia could become embroiled with Oman and the United Arab Emirates over the border in the area of the oil-rich Buraimi Oasis. If the negotiated agreement between the Saudis and the Emirates continues to be accepted by both sides, only the Omani situation would remain unsettled. But, as mentioned earlier, there is also the possibility of a large-scale Saudi-Yemeni conflict.

---

[14] "Crushing the Kurds," *Time*, March 24, 1975, p. 36.

[15] Stephen Lynton, "Iran Moves Toward 50-Mile Limit in Gulf," *Baltimore Sun*, September 30, 1973.

South Asia

On the subcontinent, Pakistan is the focal point of at least three controversies that could generate conflict—the problems of Baluchistan, Pashtoonistan, and Kashmir, each of which involves conflicting jurisdictions.

The government has tried to contain the separatist movement among Pakistan's approximately 2.5 million Baluchis, whose leaders have been fighting to maintain their regional power bases. Although internal security forces have managed to prevent widespread separatist violence, there remain various spurs to the continued life of the movement, including the involvement of outside states and their quarrels. For instance, Iraq reportedly funneled arms to the Popular Front for the Liberation of Baluchistan, a gesture linked to the strained Iraqi relations with Iran.[16]

Teheran has viewed Baluchi separation with grave concern, since "greater Baluchistan" occupies the part of Iran that controls the Straits of Hormuz. The movement does not presently seriously threaten Iran internally, because most Baluchis appear to be fairly well integrated into Iranian social and economic life. The Shah, however, probably fears that the contagion bred by a separatist success would infect the more than a million Baluchis living in Iran. Thus he has offered to help Pakistan and warned that the dismemberment of that country will not be tolerated.[17] The warning was obviously intended primarily for Pakistan's traditional enemy, India.

The Pashtoonistan problem also militates against Pakistan's fragile unity. The 8 million Pashtoons (or Pakhtuns, Pushtuns, or Pathans) living under Punjabi domination in the North West Frontier Province seem to have been comparatively content. They lacked sufficient economic and political incentives to contemplate secessionism, but in Afghanistan 40 percent of the population, including the elite, is Pashtoon. The present head of state, also a Pashtoon, has long advocated the creation of a separate state of Pashtoonistan.

In 1961 Pakistan severed diplomatic relations with Afghanistan for advocating a similar position. Rumored copper and manganese deposits in the area could add economic complications to the issue.[18] If this potential for conflict were realized, Iran would probably side with Pakistan, and India with the Pashtoons.

---

[16] R. M. Burrell and Alvin J. Cottrell, *Iran, Afghanistan, Pakistan: Tensions and Dilemmas* (London: Sage for the Georgetown Center for Strategic and International Studies, 1974), pp. 7-8.

[17] Ibid. Also, see Tahtinen, *Persian Gulf*, pp. 22-23.

[18] Burrell and Cottrell, *Iran, Afghanistan, Pakistan*, p. 41.

Pakistan's third problem is a classic case of jurisdictional conflict, which began during the partition of British India in 1948. When Kashmir's Hindu maharajah and Moslem majority refused to accede to either Pakistani or Indian sovereignty, Pashtoon and Pakistani irregulars intervened and provoked an official Indian military response. Thus began a long series of clashes, negotiations, and international mediation efforts that have left the question unresolved. Although it is under partial Indian military occupation, Kashmir has been a semi-independent state within India, enjoying autonomy not shared by other Indian provinces. It continues to be a major bone of contention in the area because Pakistan will not let the issue die.

All of these problems are compounded both by the continuing Indo-Pakistani conflict, which has several times erupted into large-scale military action, and by the presence of China, which has conducted border warfare against India. Peking's involvement has led, somewhat surprisingly, to an Iranian-Chinese relationship. Largely because of China's conflicts with India and the Soviet Union, it has extended guarantees to the regional states against nuclear blackmail by India. In such an array of interests and alignments, a local conflict could expand to include any of these powers.

Since the 1971 Indo-Pakistani War, when it gained its independence, Bangladesh has maintained uneasy relations with its neighbors and has suffered two *coups d'etat* following the assassination of its first leader, Sheikh Mujibur Rahman. The present regime, headed by Major General Ziaur Rahman, came to power on a wave of anti-Indian sentiment, partly in reaction to its former dependence on India. The government's stance toward India has since vacillated between renewed cooperation and discord, characterized by border clashes and accusations.

Various groups of insurgents, among them former Mujib loyalists, apparently receive military training in India and have regularly attacked border outposts.[19] The reported leader of the largest group of Bengali insurgents, Kadar Siddiqui, played a prominent role in the 1971 war and has allegedly vowed to avenge the death of Sheikh Mujib. Boasting some 30,000 followers, Siddiqui has recruited a large number from the Garo hill tribe, whose lands straddle the India-Bangladesh border. The Garos, Christian converts opposed to both Hindu and Moslem rule, are said to be lending their support in exchange for Siddiqui's promise of an autonomous Garoland.[20]

---

[19] William Borders, "Bangladesh Leader Accuses India of Training and Arming Guerrillas," *New York Times*, September 27, 1976.
[20] Lewis M. Simons, "Dacca Fears Step-up in Border Raids," *Washington Post*, March 23, 1976.

The short period of cooperation between Bangladesh and India seems to have resulted from congruent political objectives, primarily an effort to eliminate radical leftist forces active in southeastern Bangladesh.[21] India's participation in the antiguerrilla operations probably stemmed from its concern over the general instability in Bangladesh and its fear that the Chinese might support a radical leftist revolution there. This cooperation was abruptly halted by renewed border clashes and tension over the Farakka Barrage. The Farakka Barrage, eleven miles inside Indian territory, diverts Ganges River water from flowing into Bangladesh. A twenty-mile canal carries this water to the Hooghly River, which then washes away excessive silt deposits in Calcutta. In 1975, under pressure from India, Sheikh Mujib agreed to test the diversion for six weeks. At the end of that period, however, Bangladesh maintains that India unilaterally continued to rechannel the water, increased its flow by four times the agreed amount, and refused on-site inspections. The Zia regime in Bangladesh has blamed the diversion for a considerable loss of agricultural acreage and for the salination of canals in the south by advancing waters from the Bay of Bengal. The issue has produced a new wave of anti-Indian sentiment, and General Zia has used it to rally a semblance of national unity.[22]

Thus, the situation in Bangladesh remains indeterminate. The status of the new regime is tenuous: General Zia has had to establish his own private army, and relations with India have worsened. Under the circumstances, the various border problems stand little likelihood of being resolved. The instability invites the possibility of foreign involvement, particularly in the context of the Sino-Indian conflict. The Chinese have already shown sympathy toward Bangladesh and could extend their longstanding dispute with India to this arena.

To the southeast, in Burma, Thailand, and Malaysia, Communist groups have been exploiting the discontent of various minorities and have found enough adherents to create a continuing menace.

Burma has suffered from the disaffection of such groups as the Karen, the Mon, the Shan, and the Kachin, as well as from the two Communist movements, the so-called Red Flags, supported by the Soviet Union, and the White Flags (also called the Burma Communist Party), supported by the PRC. One White Flag group has made dangerous inroads along the Chinese-Burmese border, and, according

---

[21] Michael Chinoy, "Dacca's Strongman Consolidates," *Far Eastern Economic Review*, January 16, 1976, p. 31.
[22] Christopher Sweeney, "Small Engagement at Jamalpur," *The Guardian* (Manchester), September 19, 1976.

to the government, the movement has acquired a new dimension since the end of the Vietnam War, probably because of the transfer of arms across the border from Indochina.[23]

In Thailand, the Communists have been active in three main border areas, the northeastern Khorat Plateau, the northern tier provinces near Burma, and the southern peninsula. In the northeast provinces, which are the poorest and most isolated from the rest of the country because of rough terrain and poor communications, China, North Vietnam, and the Pathet Lao have recruited the major insurgents, the Meo tribesmen. Malaysian Communists use Thai territory as a base for attacks on Malaysia in the south, and the outlawed Communist Party of Thailand operates in the northern border regions. The Thai government's efforts to combat the insurgents have been complicated by its attempt to establish peaceful relations with its Communist neighbors.

Two separate Communist movements have mounted guerrilla campaigns in Malaysia—the Malayan Communist Party (MCP) on the peninsula and the North Kalimantan Communist Party in Sarawak. The MCP, supported mainly by the Chinese, has been conducting guerrilla operations in northern Malaysia and has perpetrated occasional acts of terrorism in Kuala Lumpur and other urban areas around the country.

In Burma, Thailand, and Malaysia, as elsewhere, the various insurgencies threaten to become an expanded conflict. They are generally assisted by foreign powers, who may want to exploit the insurgencies in these three countries as a means of expanding their regional influence. Any state considering direct military intervention, however, should undoubtedly be reminded of the American experience in Southeast Asia.

The potentially rich and powerful state of Indonesia must find a way to build a cohesive state out of its numerous ethnic and religious minorities and its many far-flung islands. Thus far, the Suharto regime has been able to meet the challenges it has faced, but there will undoubtedly be more challenges in the future, especially if externally supported national liberation groups are formed and attempt to wage militant activities against the government.

Internal dissension could also lead to external intervention in some of the island states, such as Mauritius, Sri Lanka, the Seychelles, the Comoros, and the Maldives. In Sri Lanka, the minority Tamil population has been agitating for autonomy, and the Tamil United

---

[23] "Guerrilla Activity in Burma Tied to End of Vietnam War," *New York Times*, April 1, 1976.

Liberation Front runs an office in London. The separatists could attract powerful allies among the 40 million Tamils in southern India.

This review has pointed out the large number of potential conflicts that could erupt into open hostilities along the Indian Ocean littoral. The danger is magnified by the seeming propensity of the discordant states and the guerrilla groups to seek outside support and, above all, by their success in enlisting the superpowers.

American Options in the Indian Ocean

Whether the United States or the Soviet Union bears greater responsibility for the apparent military competition in the Indian Ocean matters less at this point than this question: What is the most reasonable policy alternative for the United States? In considering the possibilities, characteristic Russian behavior should be kept in mind, especially the tendency to deploy additional combatants into the area in the wake of similar American action. A notable exception was Operation OKEAN, whose purpose was to test—and display—the Soviet capability for worldwide military operations.

The most divergent possibilities would be: (a) to withdraw unilaterally all American military forces from the Indian Ocean region, and (b) to remain in competition with the Soviet Union in the hope of retaining a position of military superiority. Either policy would undoubtedly meet determined opposition within the United States. But another option merits consideration before turning to either of these extremes.

Washington should attempt to negotiate an agreement with Moscow to avoid an arms race in the region. Because neither superpower can afford such competition at this time, both governments should be prepared to discuss the issue. Once underway, the discussions should concentrate on reducing to a minimum the military presence of both nations in the region.

Ideally, the superpowers would agree to remove all combatant vessels from the Indian Ocean. Such an agreement would appear to benefit both countries, since neither presently has an Indian Ocean fleet per se, and each would probably prefer to spend its limited military resources on other defense areas.

If the two giant powers cannot assent to zero deployment of combatants, they might agree to limit the number to perhaps six to eight and prohibit aircraft carriers and nuclear ballistic-missile submarines. It could be argued that a limitation agreement would favor the Soviet Union, which has fewer sophisticated carriers and replenishment at sea capabilities than the United States and is vulnerable to Polaris-Poseidon missiles. But the United States would also gain by avoiding an arms competition in the Indian Ocean and anywhere else. This has never been truer than at present, when the clamor for modernizing the American military, and especially the navy, often falls on ears made deaf by demands for constraints on the defense budget.

The conclusion of an arms limitation agreement could reduce the costs to the United States of expanding Diego Garcia. The navy always argued that it needed the improvements for emergency purposes, not necessarily to expand its activities in the Indian Ocean. Although it is too late to stop the construction in progress, the United States could at least limit its use of the base to reconnaissance and emergency repairs. Such use would serve the American interest, and it should appeal to Moscow as well, because it would remove large carrier forces and submarines from the area.

The United States could also reap political dividends from the littoral states by promoting a joint zone of peace or a policy of limited presence—concepts widely endorsed by these states. Because the Soviet Union has astutely limited its military presence to facilities and anchorages of low visibility, the attention of the littoral states has focused on Diego Garcia and on the overpowering presence of American carriers when they have been deployed. A change of policy, even now, might offset the loss of U.S. prestige incurred by the Diego Garcia buildup.

Negotiations with the Soviet Union would have another important benefit: while buying time to consider American options and to observe Soviet military behavior under conditions of bilateral diplomacy, the negotiations would provide a good barometer of Soviet intentions. The Soviet negotiating position might help to determine whether the United States or the U.S.S.R. has actually caused the escalation of military activity in the area. If the U.S.S.R. proves adamant in its desire to maintain a considerable presence in the region, or if it declines to make a reasonable agreement on force reductions, or if it concludes an accord only to break it in the future, then U.S. policy in the Indian Ocean would be more easily determined.

Broadly speaking, neither superpower appears prone to entangle itself in a nuclear exchange. At this point, the United States and the Soviet Union, within the context of their different political systems, seem to prefer to avoid any action that might lead to their destruction. They well know that neither would accept a conventional military defeat by the other without escalating the conflict to the nuclear level. Even the blocking of oil tanker lines would probably be considered an act of war, and the Soviet Union would probably not want to take that chance.

If Moscow should want to use force to disrupt oil supplies to the West, it would be easier to destroy the major oil fields, rather than to disrupt tanker lines, because of the proximity of the Persian Gulf to the Soviet Union. Neither the impressive weaponry of Iran nor the presence of a large American Indian Ocean fleet could effectively thwart Soviet power so close to home.

If the Kremlin should gamble that a conventional conflict would not escalate to the nuclear level, and if they should decide not to attack the oil sources, naval interdiction in the northern Atlantic Ocean and Mediterranean Sea would better suit their capabilities than action in the Indian Ocean. Indeed, in most of the decisive military categories—ranging from air cover to supply and reinforcement—the U.S.S.R. would fare better in a limited conventional war in the North Atlantic and Mediterranean areas.

For all these reasons it would appear that the wisest U.S. policy in the Indian Ocean would be to negotiate an arms limitation agreement. In the past, the Soviet Union has indicated willingness to enter into discussions of this nature, and it is possible that a fair agreement can be reached. Such an understanding might discourage the littoral states from attempting to gain a superpower patron during regional quarrels, and, conversely, it might deter Moscow and Washington from intervening in local conflicts. In every way, the likelihood of the eruption of armed hostilities should be diminished. A successful experiment with deployment limitations in the Indian Ocean might even lead to negotiations for similar restrictions elsewhere in the world.

Conclusion

As this examination has shown, any number of conflicts might erupt among the Indian Ocean littoral states, and the huge amounts of weapons needed to conduct hostilities are already in the hands of those countries. Furthermore, nothing suggests that the acquisition of arms will abate in the forseeable future.

This disconcerting situation could be immensely complicated by superpower involvement in any local conflict. Indeed, the United States and the Soviet Union frequently supply both the primary arms and the most sophisticated weapons. Thus, the resupplying of a client state during a conflict could create tensions between the superpowers.

In addition to these dangers, there is the worrisome possibility that Washington and Moscow will deploy large permanent fleets into the area, which would heighten the temptation to intervene on behalf of a client. A massive naval buildup could intensify mutual suspicions to such an extent that one side might initiate an action on the mistaken assumption that the other intended to intervene in a local dispute. And the cost to the United States—and probably to the Soviet Union as well—of building another fleet would add another strain on a budget needed to modernize other defense forces.

Consequently, it would appear to be advantageous for the superpowers to discuss establishing a zone of peace. At the least, they should be able, and willing, to arrive at a limited presence agreement. Both would profit from a limitation agreement, as would mankind as a whole.

Much has been said about the crucial geographic position of the Indian Ocean. Some have contended that the region is destined to be a chessboard for superpower rivalry, but, just because the chessmen are poised, the game need not be played. Others have argued that the dominant naval power in the region will be able to influence the policies of the littoral states, but there is no necessity for an outside naval power to dominate any region. Even if one nation should predominate, others need not be excluded from the area. Indeed, in the nuclear age, a superpower need not have large fleets and bases all over the world to be insulated from military challenges.

APPENDIX

The following tables are intended to give specific details on the weapons inventories of the Indian Ocean states discussed in the preceding text. Such tables alone cannot reflect the full military potential of a nation because they omit the vital human element. They do, however, support the conclusion drawn in the text that the Indian Ocean region is far from being a power vacuum in the usual sense of the term.

Table A-1
AIRCRAFT IN INDIAN OCEAN LITTORAL STATES

Country and Aircraft Type	1968–69	1976–77
AUSTRALIA		
Air Force		
F111-C	—	24
Aermacchi MB-326 (light strike)	16 (59 on order)	—
Canberra B-20 (light bomber)	40	13 (9 more in storage)
Mirage III-0 (jet fighter)	80	48 (67 more in storage)
Sabre (fighter)	60	—
P-3B Orion	10	10 (8 P-3C on order)
SP-2H Neptune	12	12
Total	218	107
Navy		
A-4G Skyhawk	10	8
S-2E Tracker	14	13 (mostly destroyed in recent fire)
HS-748	—	2
Total	24	23
Composite	242	130
BANGLADESH		
MiG-21	—	9[a]
BURMA		
AT-33 (counterinsurgency)	—	5
F-86F Sabre (fighter-bomber)	—	some
Vampire (fighter-bomber)	5	some
T-33 (armed trainer)	12	—
Sea Fury (fighter-bomber)	3	—
Vampire (armed trainer)	6	—
Total	26	10[a]

Table A-1 (continued)

Country and Aircraft Type	1968–69	1976–77
ETHIOPIA		
A-37B (counterinsurgency)	—	(12 on order)
T-28A (reconnaissance)	6 [b]	5
B-2 Canberra (light bomber)	6 [b]	4
F-86F (fighter)	12 [b]	11
Saab 17 (ground attack)	8 [b]	—
F-5A/E (fighter)	8 [b]	16 (8 on order)
RT-33 (reconnaissance)	3 [b]	—
Total	43 [b]	36
INDIA		
Air Force		
Convair B-24 (maritime reconnaissance)	7	—
Iskra	—	(90 on order)
Canberra PR-57 (reconnaissance)	8	12
HF-24 Marut 1A (fighter-bomber)	—	80 (55 on order)
Su-7B (fighter-bomber)	6	130
Canberra B(1) (light bomber)	45	80
MiG-21 (interceptor)	80	275 (110 on order)
Hunter F-56 (fighter, ground attack)	150	130
Gnat Mark 1 (interceptor)	150	250 (100 on order)
Mystere IV (fighter-bomber)	60	—
Vampire	—	—
Ouragan	(50 in reserve)	—
Total	506	957
Naval Air Force		
Il-38	—	3
Sea Hawk	30	25
Alizé	12	12
L-1049 Super Constellation	—	3
Total	42	43
Composite	548	1,000

Table A-1 (continued)

Country and Aircraft Type	1968–69	1976–77
INDONESIA		
MiG-15	} 55	} (40 in storage)
MiG-17		
MiG-19		(35 in storage)
MiG-21	16	(15 in storage)
Il-28 (light bomber)	20	(10 in storage)
F-51D Mustang (light strike)	20	14
Tu-16 (medium bomber)	25	(22 in storage)
B-25 Mitchell ⎫ (light	} 18	—
B-26 Invader ⎭ bombers)		—
CA-27 Avon-Sabre	—	16
HU-16 ⎫	—	5
C-47 ⎬ Maritime reconnaissance	—	6
Nomad ⎭	—	6
Total	154	47 [a]
IRAN		
Air Force		
F-4D (fighter-bomber)	36	32
F-4E (fighter-bomber)	—	141 (36 on order)
F-5A (fighter-ground attack)	—	12
F-5E (fighter-ground attack)	90	100 (41 on order)
F-14A Tomcat	—	15 (65 on order)
RF-4E (reconnaissance)	—	4 (12 on order)
RF-5A (reconnaissance)	—	13
P-3 Orion	—	(6 on order)
F-86 (interceptor)	60	—
Tactical reconnaissance aircraft	16	—
Total	202	317
Naval Air Force		
P-3F Orion	—	6
Composite	202	323
IRAQ		
MiG-23	—	40
Su-7B	20	50

Country and Aircraft Type	1968–69	1976–77
MiG-17	} 45	30
MiG-19		20
Hunter	50	50
MiG-21	60	90
Tu-16 (bomber)	8	9
Il-28 (light bomber)	10	10
T-52 jet Provost (light strike)	20	—
Total	213	299
KENYA		
F-5E/F	—	(12 on order)
BAC-167	—	5
Hunter	—	5
SA-Bulldog (counter-insurgency)	—	5
Total	—	15
KUWAIT		
Hunter FGA57	—[c]	4
T-67 (fighter-ground attack)	—[c]	5
Lightning F-53 (interceptor)	—[c]	10
T-55 (interceptor)	—[c]	2
BAC-167 Strikemaster Mk 83 (counter-insurgency)	—[c]	12
Mirage F-1	—[c]	(20 on order)
A-4M Skyhawk	—[c]	(36 on order)
TA-4K	—[c]	(6 on order)
Total	—[c]	33
MALAGASY REPUBLIC	—	—
MALAYSIA		
F-5E	—	14
CA-27 Sabre fighters	—	16[d]
CL-41G Tebuan (light strike)	20	20
Total	20	50

Country and Aircraft Type	1968–69	1976–77
MOZAMBIQUE		
MiG fighters	—	some
OMAN		
Jaguar	—[c]	(12 on order)
BAC-167 (ground attack)	—[c]	15
Hunter (fighter, ground attack)	—[c]	29
Total	—[c]	44
PAKISTAN		
Air Force		
Atlantic	—	3
Mirage III (interceptor, fighter-bomber)	14	—
Mirage III EP/DP	—	28
Mirage V	—	28
MiG-19 (interceptor)	40	—
MiG-19/F6 (fighter, ground attack)	—	80
B-57B Canberra (light bomber)	20	15
Il-28 (light bomber)	4	—
F-104 (interceptor)	12	—
F-86 Sabre (fighter-bomber)	140	60
RB-57 ⎫		—
Mirage IIIR ⎬ reconnaissance	20	3 (10 on order)
RT-33A ⎭		—
Total	250	217
Naval Air Force		
Albatross	some	—
SAUDI ARABIA		
F-86 Sabre	11[e]	—
F-5E (fighter-bomber)	—	30 (100 on order)
BAC-167 (counter-insurgency)	—	30
Lightning F52/3/4 (interceptor)	24	37

50

Country and Aircraft Type	1968–69	1976–77
Mirage V ES/DS	—	(38 on order)
Hunter	4	—
Total	39	97
SINGAPORE		
Hunter FGA/FR74/T75	(20 on order)[b]	42
A-4	—	40
BAC-167 (counter-insurgency)	10 (6 on order)[b]	15
Total	10[b]	97
SOMALIA		
MiG-15	} 18[b]	} 44
MiG-17		
Il-28	—	10
MiG-21	—	12
Total	18[b]	66[a]
SOUTH AFRICA		
Air Force		
Mirage F1AZ	—	(32 on order)
Mirage F1CZ	—	16
Mirage III-DZ	—	14
Mirage III-EZ (fighter-bomber)	20[g]	16
Mirage III-CZ (interceptor)	16	
Mirage III-RZ	—	} 27
Mirage BZ	—	
Piaggio P-166S Albatross	—	20
B(I) Mark 12 Canberra	—	6
T Mk 4	—	3
Shackleton (maritime reconnaissance)	7	7
F-86 Sabre	—	15[f]
B-12 Canberra (light bomber)	9	—
Mark 50 Buccaneer (light bomber)	15	9
Total	67	253

Table A-1 (continued)

Country and Aircraft Type	1968–69	1976–77
Citizen Air Force and Reserves		
Sabre Mark 6	30	—
Vampire	16	—
Harvard	100	145
Impala I/II	—	36 (30 on order)
Total	146	181
Composite	213	434

SRI LANKA (CEYLON)

MiG-17	—c	5

TANZANIA

MiG-21	—	15
MiG-19 (F-6)	—	8
MiG-17	—	10
Total	—	33

THAILAND

F-5E ⎫	—	24 (16 F-5E on order)
F-5A ⎬(fighter-bomber)	⎱ 25	
F-5B ⎭		2
RT-33A (tactical reconnaissance)	6	4
RF-5A (reconnaissance)	—	4
T-33 (reconnaissance)	—	20
F-86F (fighter-bomber)	40	—
F-86L (fighter-interceptor)	20	—
T-28D (counterinsurgency)	40	36
T-6 (counterinsurgency)	20	30
OV-10 (counterinsurgency)	—	32
AU-23A (counterinsurgency)	—	11 (20 on order)
A-37 (counterinsurgency)	—	16
Total	151	179

Table A-1 (continued)

Country and Aircraft Type	1968–69	1976–77
UNITED ARAB EMIRATES		
Mirage V	—c	14
Hunter	—c	12
MB-326 (counter- insurgency)	—c	8
Total	—c	34
YEMEN (NORTH)		
MiG-17 (fighter-bomber)	—c	12
II-28 (light bomber)	—c	16
Total	—c	28 h
YEMEN (SOUTH)		
MiG-17	—c	15
MiG-21	—c	12
Total	—c	27 h

a Spaces are short and not all equipment is serviceable.
b Figures from 1970-71.
c Not available.
d Being withdrawn.
e Obsolescent.
f Being replaced by Mirage F1AZ.
g With AS-20, AS-30 ASM.
h Some aircraft are believed to be in storage.
Source: *Military Balance 1968-69, 1970-71*, and *1976-77.*

Table A-2

HELICOPTERS IN INDIAN OCEAN LITTORAL STATES

Country and Helicopter Type	1968–69	1976–77	
AUSTRALIA			
Air Force			
UH-1H Iroquois	—	47	
UH-1B Iroquois	2 squadrons	—	
CH-47 Chinook	—	12	
Total	2 squadrons	59	
Army			
Sioux	} 50	—	
Alouette III		—	
Bell 47	—	29	
Bell 206B-1	—	44	(9 on order)
Total	50	73	
Navy			
Wessex Mark 31	1 squadron	4	
Bell UH-1H	—	4	
Bell 206B	—	2	
Total	1 squadron	10	
Composite	4 squadrons	142	
BANGLADESH			
Alouette III	—	5	
Wessex	—	2	
Mi-8	—	4	
Total	—	11	
BURMA			
KB-47G	—	13	
HH-43	—	12	
Shawnee	—	—	
UH-1	—	18	
Vertol	} 40	—	
Sioux		—	
Huskie		—	
Alouette III		13	
Total	40	56	

54

Country and Helicopter Type	1968–69	1976–77
ETHIOPIA		
Alouette	3[a]	—
AB-204B	—	10
Bell UH-1H	—	6
Total	3[a]	16
INDIA		
Air Force		
Mi-8	—	35
Mi-4	90	100
Alouette III (Chetek)	50	120
AB-47	—	12
Bell-47	4	—
S-55	6	—
Total	150	267
Navy		
Hughes-300	—	4
Alouette III	some	22
Sea King	—	12
Total	some	38
Army		
Alouette III	—	some
SA-315 Cheetah	—	25 (75 on order)
Composite	150 +	330 +
INDONESIA		
Bell-206B	—	(2 on order)
Alouette III[b]	—	17
S-61A	—	1
Bell 47-G	—	4 (3 on order)
Mi-6 Hook	some	(9 in storage)
Mi-4	6	(20 in storage)
UH-34D	—	4
Bell 204B	—	5
Other	some	—
Total	41	31

Country and Helicopter Type	1968–69	1976–77
IRAN		
Army		
AH-1J	—	60 (142 on order)
Bell 214A	—	100 (187 on order)
Huskie	—	20
AB-205A	—	52
CH-47C	—	15
Total	—	247
Navy		
S-65A (antisubmarine)	—	6 (6 on order)
AB-205A	—	5
AB-206A	—	14
AB-212	—	6
SH-3D	—	10
Total	—	41
Air Force		
Whirlwind	} 25	—
Huskie		10
AB-205	—	45
AB-206A	—	70
AB-212	—	5
CH-47C	—	5 (22 on order)
Super Frelon	—	16
Bell 214C	—	(39 on order)
Total	25	151
Composite	25	439
IRAQ		
Mi-1	—	4
Mi-4	9	35
Mi-6	—	16
Mi-8	—	30
Alouette III	—	40 (20 on order)
Wessex	11	9
Total	20	134

Table A-2 (continued)

Country and Helicopter Type	1968–69	1976–77
KENYA		
Alouette II	—	3
Bell 47-G	—	2
Total	—	5
KUWAIT		
AB-204B	—c	2
AB-205	—c	4
Whirlwind	—c	2
Gazelle	—c	20
Puma	—c	10
Total	—c	38
MALAGASY REPUBLIC		
Alouette II and III	—	3
Bell 47-G	—	1
Other	1a	—
Total	1a	4
MALAYSIA		
Bell 47-G	—	9
Alouette III	24	25
S61-A	10	14
Total	34	48
MOZAMBIQUE	—	—
OMAN		
AB-205	—c	20
AB-214A	—c	(5 on order)
AB-206A	—c	2
Total	—c	22

57

Country and Helicopter Type	1968–69	1976–77
PAKISTAN		
Air Force		
SA-330 Puma	—	1
Super Frelon	—	(4 on order)
Alouette III	⎫	14
Bell-47	⎬ 25	12
Kaman-43B	⎭	—
HH-43B	—	10
Total	25	37
Navy		
UH-19 (SAR)	some	2
Sea King	—	2 (4 on order)
Total	some	4
Army		
Bell 47-G	—	20
Mi-8	—	12
Alouette III	—	20
Total	—	52
Composite	25 +	93
SAUDI ARABIA		
AB-206	⎫ 20	16
AB-205	⎭	24
Alouette III	2	12 (more on order)
AB-204	—	1
Total	22	53
SINGAPORE		
Alouette III (search and rescue)	8[a]	7
SOMALIA		
Mi-2	—	⎫
Mi-4	—	⎬ In one squadron
Mi-8	—	⎭

Table A-2 (continued)

Country and Helicopter Type	1968–69	1976–77
SOUTH AFRICA		
SA-330 Puma	—	25
Alouette III	—	40
Alouette	50	—
S-51	⎱ 6	—
S-55	⎰	—
Wasp (naval-assigned)	4	12
Super Frelon (SA-321L)	16	15
Other	4	—
Total	80	92
SRI LANKA (CEYLON)		
Jet Ranger	—c	7
KA-26	—c	2
Bell 47-G2	—c	6
Total	—c	15
TANZANIA		
AB-206	—	2
Bell 47-G	—	2
Total	—	4
THAILAND		
Air Force		
FH-1100	—	16
UH-1H	—	50
Bell 206	—	3
H-19 Chicksaw (UH-19)	—	13
OH-23F	—	6
CH-34C	22	40
Huskie	—	3
CH-19	⎱	—
S-51	⎬ 38	—
S-55	⎰	—
UH-1B/D	—	90
OH-13	—	24
CH-47	—	4
Total	60	249

Table A-2 (continued)

Country and Helicopter Type	1968–69	1976–77
UNITED ARAB EMIRATES		
AB-205	—c	6
AB-206	—c	6
Alouette III	—c	5
Puma	—c	5
Bell 212	—c	3
Total	—c	25
YEMEN (NORTH)		
AB-205	—c	some
Mi-4	—c	some
YEMEN (SOUTH)		
Mi-4	—c	some
Mi-8	—c	8
Total	—c	8+

a Figures from 1970-71.

b Including a few Alouette II.

c Not available.

Source: *The Military Balance 1968-69, 1970-71,* and *1976-77.*

Table A-3

NAVAL CRAFT IN INDIAN OCEAN LITTORAL STATES

Country and Naval Craft Type	1968–69	1976–77
AUSTRALIA		
Aircraft carrier	—	1
Submarines (Oberon-class fleet submarines)	3	4 (2 on order)
Guided missile destroyers	3	—
Gun destroyers	3	3 (2 on order)
ASW destroyers (with Tartar SAM and Ikara ASW missiles)	—	3
Frigates (some with Seacat SAM and Ikara ASW missiles)	4	6
Light fleet carrier (ASW)	1	—
Patrol boats	—	12
Coastal minehunters	—	2
Coastal minesweeper	6	1
Fast troop transport	1	—
Landing craft	—	6
Support ships	18	2
Total	39	40
BANGLADESH		
Patrol craft	—	4
Armed river patrol boats	—	3
Support vessel	—	1
Total	—	8
BURMA		
Frigates	1	2
Motor torpedo boats (less than 100 tons)	5	5
Motor gunboats (less than 100 tons)	—	
River patrol gunboats (less than 100 tons)	—	35
Gunboats	37	36
Coastal escorts	2	4
Escort minesweeper	1	—
Transports	—	10
Auxiliaries	2	—
Total	48	92

Table A-3 (continued)

Country and Naval Craft Type	1968–69	1976–77
ETHIOPIA		
Kraljevica-class patrol boat	—	1
Patrol boats	5 [a]	5
Coastal patrol craft (less than 50 tons)	—	4
Motor torpedo boats (less than 100 tons)	2 [a]	—
Coastal minesweeper	—	1
Landing craft	4 [a]	4
Training ship (ex-U.S. seaplane tender)	1 [a]	1
Total	12 [a]	16
INDIA		
Aircraft carrier (16,000 tons; capacity 21 aircraft)	1	1
Submarines (ex-Soviet F-class)	1	8
Cruisers	2	2
Destroyers	3	3
Anti-aircraft frigates	3	—
ASW frigates	5	—
Frigates (3 with Seacat SAM, 10 Petya-class, 9 group, 1 anti-aircraft, 1 training)	—	26
Destroyer escorts (including 1 ex-Soviet Petya-class)	3	—
Patrol boats (Osa-class)	—	8
Patrol craft	2	15
Minesweepers	—	4
Coastal minesweepers	4	—
Inshore minesweepers	2	4
Other escort vessels	2	—
Seaward defense boats	3	—
Landing ship	1	1
Landing craft	3	6 [b]
Survey ships	4	—
Others	5	—
Total	44	78

Country and Naval Craft Type	1968–69	1976–77
INDONESIA		
Submarines (ex-Soviet W-class)	6	3
Heavy cruiser (ex-Soviet Sverdlov-class)	1	—
Destroyers (ex-Soviet Skory-class)	7	—
Frigates (some of which are ex-Soviet Riga-class and ex-U.S. Jones-class)	11	9
Corvettes	3	(3 on order)
Komar-class missile patrol boats (with Styx SSM)	12	9
Motor gunboats	21	—
Motor torpedo boats (P-6 type; less than 100 tons)	6	—
Motor torpedo boats	7	—
Patrol vessels	11	40
Coastal minesweepers	11	⎫
Fleet minesweepers (including ex-Soviet T-43 class)	6	⎬ 14 ⎭
Coastal escorts (including ex-Soviet Kronstadt-class)	12	20
Submarine support ships	3	—
Landing ships	7	—
Landing craft	7	—
HQ support ships	—	3
Amphibious warfare vessels	—	10
Others	50	—
Total	181	108 c
IRAN		
Destroyers (with Seacat and Standard SAM)	—	3
Escort destroyers	2	—
Frigates (with MK-2 Seakiller SSM and Seacat SAM)	—	4
Corvettes (ex-U.S. patrol frigates)	—	4
SRN-6 hovercraft	—	8
Wellington BH-7 hovercraft	—	6
Kaman attack craft with Harpoon SSM	—	(4 on order)
Patrol boats	24	25
Inshore minesweepers	2	2
Coastal minesweepers	4	3

Table A-3 (continued)

Country and Naval Craft Type	1968–69	1976–77
Landing ships	—	2
Landing craft	3	2
Logistic support ships	—	2
Other escorts	4	—
Other ships	6	—
Total	45	61
IRAQ		
SOI submarine chasers	—	3
Osa-class fast patrol boats (with Styx SSM)	—	8
P-6 torpedo boats	—	12
Motor torpedo boats	some	—
Patrol boats (under 100 tons)	some	3
Minesweepers	—	2
Total	some	28
KENYA		
Motor gunboats (some with 40 mm. Bofors guns)	—	7
Patrol boats	3 a	—
Seaward defense boat	1 a	—
Total	4 a	7
KUWAIT		
Inshore patrol boats	— d	12
Patrol launches	— d	16
Landing craft	— d	3
Total	— d	31
MALAGASY REPUBLIC		
Patrol vessels	2 a	8
Transport	—	1
Tender	1 a	—
Marine coy	—	1
Training ship	1 a	—
Total	4 a	10

64

Table A-3 (continued)

Country and Naval Craft Type	1968–69	1976–77
MALAYSIA		
ASW frigate (with Seacat SAM)	1	1
Fast patrol boats (less than 100 tons; with SS-11/12 and Exocet SSM)	4	8 (4 on order)
Other patrol boats (less than 100 tons)	24	28
Coastal minesweepers	6	6
Inshore minesweepers	2	—
Riverine craft	—	12
Support ships	3	—
Training frigate	—	1
Total	40	56
MOZAMBIQUE	—	—
OMAN		
Fast patrol boats	—d	3 (4 on order)
Patrol craft	—d	3
Small landing craft	—d	3
Total	—d	9
PAKISTAN		
Submarines	1	3 (3 on order)
Midget submarines (Italian SX-404 class)	—	6
Large destroyers (ex-British battle-, CH-, and CR-class)	2	4
ASW frigates	2	4
Destroyer escorts	3	—
Fast patrol boats (ex-Chinese Hu Chwan and Shanghai-class)	4	17
Small patrol boats (less than 100 tons)	2	—
Coastal minesweepers	8	8
Support ships	8	—
Light cruiser trainer	—	1
Total	30	43

Table A-3 (continued)

Country and Naval Craft Type	1968–69	1976–77
SAUDI ARABIA		
Fast patrol boats (including Jaguar-class and ex-U.S. Coast Guard cutter)	—	3 (6 on order)
Mine countermeasures craft	—	(4 on order)
Coastal patrol craft	some	—
Coastal escort vessel	1	—
Landing craft	—	(4 on order)
Total	some	3
SINGAPORE		
Jaguar-class fast patrol boats (with Gabriel SSM)	—	6
Motor gunboats	—	6
Patrol boats	some	—
Patrol craft	2	5
LST (landing ship, tank)	—	1
Landing craft	—	4
Total	2+	22
SOMALIA		
Fast patrol boats (Osa-class with Styx SSM)	—	2
P-4 motor torpedo boats (ex-Soviet)	—	6
P-6 motor torpedo boats (ex-Soviet)	—	4
Patrol boats	6 [a]	—
Landing craft (medium, ex-Soviet T-4 class)	—	4
Total	6 [a]	16
SOUTH AFRICA		
Submarines (Daphne-class)	(3 on order)	3 (2 Agosta-class on order)
Destroyers	2	2
ASW frigates	6 (3 without ASW)	5 (2 on order)
Corvettes (with Gabriel SSM)	—	(6 on order)
Fast patrol guided-missile boats	—	(3 on order)

Table A-3 (continued)

Country and Naval Craft Type	1968–69	1976–77
Patrol craft (ex-British Ford-class)	—	5
Coastal minesweepers	10	10
Escort minesweeper	—	1
Seaward defense boats	5	—
Training ship	1	—
Auxiliaries	3	—
Total	27	26
SRI LANKA (CEYLON)		
Frigate	—[d]	1
Fast patrol boat (Osa-class)	—[d]	1
Fast gunboats	—[d]	5
Small patrol craft	—[d]	23
Total	—[d]	30
TANZANIA		
Patrol boats	4[a]	—
Hu Chwan-class hydrofoils	—	4
Shanghai-class motor gunboats	—	6
Fast patrol boats	—	6
Total	4[a]	16
THAILAND		
Frigates	4	7
Destroyer escort	1	—
Fast patrol guided-missile boats	—	(3 on order)
Armored gunboats	2	—
Gunboats (less than 100 tons)	—	26
Mine-warfare ships	—	18
Coastal minesweepers (less than 100 tons)	6	—
Escort minesweeper	1	—
River patrol boats	—	28
Patrol vessels	20	14
Landing ships	} 13	—
Landing craft		9
Total	47	102

Table A-3 (continued)

Country and Naval Craft Type	1968–69	1976–77
UNITED ARAB EMIRATES		
Large patrol craft	—d	6
Coastal patrol craft	—d	14
Powered dinghies	—d	4
Total	—d	24
YEMEN (NORTH)		
P-4-class fast patrol boats (ex-Soviet)	—d	5
YEMEN (SOUTH)		
SOI-class submarine chasers (ex-Soviet)	—d	2
P-6-class torpedo boats (ex-Soviet)	—d	2
Minesweepers (ex-British Ham-class)	—d	3
Small patrol craft	—d	15
Landing craft (medium)	—d	2
Total	—d	24

a Figures from 1970-71.

b Five of which are Polnocny-class.

c Some equipment and ships are nonoperational due to lack of spares.

d Not available.

Note: *Jane's Fighting Ships, 1976-77* defines *light cruisers* as major surface ships above 5,000 tons; *destroyers,* 3,000 tons and over including original destroyers; *frigates,* 1,100 to 3,000 tons; and *corvettes,* 500 to 1,100 tons.

Source: *The Military Balance 1968-69, 1970-71,* and *1976-77.*

Table A-4

MILITARY MANPOWER IN INDIAN OCEAN LITTORAL STATES 1976–1977

	Army	Navy	Air Force
Australia	31,600	16,200	21,550
Bangladesh	59,000	1,000	3,000
Burma	153,000	9,000	7,500
Ethiopia	47,000	1,500	2,300
India	913,000	42,500	100,000
Indonesia	180,000	38,000	28,000
Iran	200,000	18,500	81,500
Iraq	140,000	3,000	15,000
Kenya	6,500	340	760
Kuwait	8,500	200	1,000
Malagasy Republic	4,000	600	160
Malaysia	52,500	4,800	5,000
Mozambique	10,000[a]	—	unknown
Oman	13,200	400	550
Pakistan	400,000	11,000	17,000
Saudi Arabia	40,000	1,500	10,000
Singapore	25,000	3,000	3,000
Somalia	22,000	300	2,700
South Africa	38,000	5,000	8,500
Sri Lanka (Ceylon)	8,900	2,400	2,300
Tanzania	13,000	600	1,000
Thailand	141,000	27,000	42,000
United Arab Emirates	18,800	800	1,800
Yemen (North)	37,000	500	1,500
Yemen (South)	19,000	300	2,000

[a] Estimated number of Frelimo troops at time of independence, June 1975.
Source: *The Military Balance 1976-77.*

Table A-5
TANKS IN INDIAN OCEAN LITTORAL STATES

Country and Tank Type	1968–69	1976–77
AUSTRALIA		
Centurion	1 regiment	143
Leopard (medium)	—	(87 on order)
Total	1 regiment	143
BANGLADESH		
T-54 (medium)	—	30
Total	—	30
BURMA		
Comet (light)	some	some
ETHIOPIA		
M-60 (medium)	—	24 (24 on order)
M-24 Chaffee (light)	} 50 [a]	—
M-41 Walker Bulldog		54
Total	50 [a]	78
INDIA		
T-55 (medium)	—	} 1,000
T-54 (medium)	} 400 [b]	
T-34 (medium)		—
Vijayanta (medium)	50	700 [c]
Centurion (medium)	220	180
Sherman (medium)	250	—
Stuart (light)	50	—
AMX-13 (light)	90	—
PT-76 (light)	100	150
Total	1,160	2,030 [c]
INDONESIA		
Stuart (light)	—	some
AMX-13 (light)	approximately 7 battalions with either	50
PT-76 (light)		75
Total	—	125 +

Country and Tank Type	1968–69	1976–77
IRAN		
M-24	some	—
Chieftain	—	500 (1,480 on order)
M-47 and 48	some	400
M-60A1 (medium)	some	460
Scorpion (light)	—	(250 on order)
Total	some	1,360
IRAQ		
Centurion	55	—
T-62	—	⎫
T-54 and 55	300	⎬ 1,200
T-34 (medium)	180	90
Chaffee (light)	40	—
PT-76 (light)	—	100
Total	575	1,390
KENYA	—	—
KUWAIT		
Vickers (medium)	—d	50
Centurion (medium)	—d	50
Chieftain	—d	(165 on order)
Total	—d	100
MALAGASY REPUBLIC	—	—
MALAYSIA	—	—
MOZAMBIQUE	—	—
OMAN	—d	—

Table A-5 (continued)

Country and Tank Type	1968–69	1976–77
PAKISTAN		
Chinese T-60	—	some
T-59 (medium)	—	700
T-55 (medium)	—	50
M-4 Sherman		some
M-47 Patton (medium)	4 armored	250
M-48 Patton (medium)	brigades	
Chinese T-59		—
M-24 Chaffee (light)	some in recon-	50
M-41 Bulldog (light)	naissance regiment	—
Total	some	1,050+
SAUDI ARABIA		
M-24	some	—
AMX-30	—	300 (100 on order)
AMX-13	some	—
M-47 (medium)	some	25
M-41 (light)	some	60
M-60 (medium)	—	(250 on order)
Scorpion (light)	—	(250 on order)
Total	some	385
SINGAPORE		
AMX-13	80[a][e]	75
SOMALI REPUBLIC		
T-34 (medium)	150[a][f]	200
T-54/55 (medium)	—	50
Total	150[a][f]	250
SOUTH AFRICA		
Centurion 5	100	141
Sherman	50	—
Comet		20
Total	150	161

72

Table A-5 (continued)

Country and Tank Type	1968–69	1976–77
SRI LANKA (CEYLON)	—d	—
TANZANIA		
Chinese T-60	—	some
Chinese T-59 (medium)	—	20
Chinese T-62 (light)	12a	14
Total	12a	34+
THAILAND		
M-24 Chaffee	some	20
M-41 Bulldog	some	175
Total	some	195
UNITED ARAB EMIRATES		
Scorpion (light)	—d	27
YEMEN (NORTH)		
T-34 (medium)	—d	30
YEMEN (SOUTH)		
T-34 (medium)	—d	} 200
T-54 (medium)	—d	

a Figures from 1970-71.
b Not yet considered operational.
c Figure is approximate.
d Not available.
e To be operational in 1971.
f Only about half are likely to be serviceable.
Source: *The Military Balance 1968-69, 1970-71,* and *1976-77;* and *Jane's Weapons Systems 1976.*

Table A-6

ARMORED PERSONNEL CARRIERS IN
INDIAN OCEAN LITTORAL STATES

Country and Armored Personnel Carrier Type	1968–69	1976–77
AUSTRALIA		
M-113	—	753
BANGLADESH	—	—
BURMA	—	—
ETHIOPIA		
Various types	40[a]	—
M-113	—	90[b] (more on order)
Total	40[a]	90[b]
INDIA		
OT-62	—	⎫
OT-64 (2A)	—	700
MK-2 and 4A	—	⎭
Total	—	700
INDONESIA		
Saracen	—	some
BTR-40	—	130
Total	—	130+
IRAN		
M-113	some	⎫
BTR-50 and 60	—	2,000
BTR-152	some	—
Total	some	2,000

Table A-6 (continued)

Country and Armored Personnel Carrier Type	1968–69	1976–77
IRAQ		
BTR-60	—	} 1,600
BTR-152	—	
BMP-76	—	
Total	—	1,600
KENYA	—	—
KUWAIT		
Saracen	—c	130
MALAGASY REPUBLIC		
M-3A1	—	some
MALAYSIA		
Commando	—	200 (100 on order)
AML/M-3	—	140
Total	—	340
MOZAMBIQUE	—	—
OMAN	—c	—
PAKISTAN		
M-113	—	400
SAUDI ARABIA		
Unknown type	—	(250 on order)
SINGAPORE		
V-200 Commando	—	250
M-113	—	250
Total	—	500

Table A-6 (continued)

Country and Armored Personnel Carrier Type	1968–69	1976–77
SOMALI REPUBLIC		
Various types (including BTR-152)	60 [a]	—
BTR-40	—	60
BTR-152	—	250
Total	60 [a]	310
SOUTH AFRICA		
Ratel	—	} 250
Saracen	some	
Total	some	250
SRI LANKA (CEYLON)		
BTR-152	— [c]	10
TANZANIA		
BTR-152	15 [a]	some
BTR-40	some [a]	some
Total	15+	some
THAILAND		
M-113	—	200
UNITED ARAB EMIRATES	— [c]	—
YEMEN (NORTH)		
BTR-40	— [c]	100
YEMEN (SOUTH)	— [c]	—

[a] Figures from 1970-71.
[b] Figure is approximate.
[c] Not available.
Source: *The Military Balance 1968-69, 1970-71,* and *1976-77.*

Table A-7

CHARACTERISTICS OF MAJOR AIRCRAFT
IN INDIAN OCEAN LITTORAL STATES

Type	Characteristics
F-111	A two-seat multipurpose fighter-bomber designed to fly at supersonic speeds at sea level and to take off from short, rough airfields. It carries a full range of modern warloads of conventional and nuclear weapons, modern air-to-surface tactical weapons, and such air-to-air missiles as the Phoenix. Variants have also been constructed for ECM reconnaissance and strategic nuclear missions. Speed: Mach 2.2. Ordnance: almost 16 tons. Range with maximum internal fuel: 3,165 miles.
P-3 Orion	A four turboprop-engined ASW aircraft equipped with the most modern and sophisticated submarine detection devices. These include tactical display, 360 degree radar, trail detector, sonobuoy signal receivers, indicator and recorder, acoustic processor, magnetic anomaly detector, and a digital computer that integrates all tracking and targeting information. The P-3 also carries various combinations of bombs, mines, conventional and nuclear depth bombs, torpedoes, rockets, sonobuoys, sound signals, and marine markers. Maximum speed: 473 mph. Normal patrol speed: 237 mph. Ordnance: 10 tons. Maximum mission radius: 2,383 miles.
Il-38	This is the ASW-converted version of the Soviet-built Il-18 airliner—a conversion similar to Lockheed's transformation of the Electra transport into the P-3 Orion. Carrying a magnetic anomaly detector, weapons (presumably ASW), and electronic equipment, the Il-38 is the principal shore-based maritime patrol aircraft of the Soviet naval air force. Maximum cruising speed: 400 mph. Maximum range: 4,500 miles.
F-14	The most modern multirole fighter designed for three purposes: clearing contested airspace and protecting the strike force, defense of carrier task forces, and secondary ground attack missions. The F-14 can work in cooperation with early warning aircraft, surface ships, and fighter escorts in carrying out its various missions, and has great agility for close-in air-to-air combat. It can carry a 20-mm. gun, four Sparrow or Phoenix air-to-air missiles that can be launched simultaneously against four separate targets, and various combinations of other missiles and bombs. Speed: Mach 2.3. Ordnance: 7.3 tons. Combat radius: not available.
F-4E	The F-4E uses highly sophisticated ECM equipment, computers, and radar in its role as a long-range all-

Type	Characteristics
	weather attack fighter. Until the recent emergence of the F-14, the F-4 was considered to be the best operational American missile-armed aircraft. The F-4 carries 4 Sparrow plus 4 Sidewinder air-to-air missiles plus a variety of other loads such as bombs, mines, napalm, Bullpup air-to-surface missiles, rockets, and smoke bombs. Speed: Mach 2+. Ordnance: 8 tons. Combat radius: 900-1,000 miles.
MiG-23	A tactical air superiority fighter designed to intercept fast-strike aircraft. Little is certain about its avionics, but the MiG-23 is believed to have several of the following features: radar, ECM equipment, and possibly "snap-down" missiles for use against low-flying attack aircraft. It can carry a variety of armament. Speed: Mach 2.3. Ordnance: 4 tons. Combat radius: 600 miles.
Su-7	After 1961, the Su-7 became the standard tactical fighter bomber of the Soviet air force. Little information is available on its avionics. Speed (with external stores): Mach 1.2. Ordnance: 2.2 tons. Combat radius: 200-300 miles.
F-5A/B/E	A light tactical fighter suitable for a wide range of combat duties. Though powered by two turbojets, the F-5 is capable of takeoff, climb to altitude, completion of a mission, and return to base on one engine. The F-5 normally carries two Sidewinder missiles, two 20-mm. guns, and a variety of other warloads, including a 2,000 lb. bomb suspended from the center pylon, four air-to-air missiles, combination of bombs, air-to-surface rockets, gun packs or external fuel tanks. Maximum speed: Mach 1.4. Maximum military load: 6,200 lbs. Combat radius: with maximum payload plus five minutes combat: 195 miles; with maximum fuel, two 530 lb. bombs plus five minutes combat: 558 miles. F-5E is the successor and improved version of F-5A with added emphasis on maneuverability.
Mirage III-E	A long-range fighter/bomber/intruder, variants of which have been manufactured for reconnaissance purposes (Mirage III-R) and for all-weather-interceptor and day ground-attack-fighter roles (Mirage III-C). Its ground-attack armament normally consists of two 1,000 lb. bombs plus two 30-mm. cannons, or an AS.30 air-to-surface missile, or rocket pods plus extra fuel. As an interceptor, Mirage III carries one Matra R.530 all-weather air-to-air missile with radar or infrared homing heads plus optional guns and two Sidewinder missiles. Maximum speed: Mach 2.2. Ordnance: 1 ton. Combat radius, ground attack: 560-745 miles.

Type	Characteristics
BAC-167	A light tactical support aircraft especially useful for counterinsurgency combat operations. It carries a variety of armament including machine guns, rockets, ballistic and retarded bombs, napalm, and gunpacks. Speed: 518 mph. Ordnance: 1.5 tons. Combat radius: 145-575 miles.
Hunter Mk-9	A single-seat fighter aircraft with automatic gun-ranging radar with scanner and gyro-gunsight. Hunter can carry a variety of rockets and other weapons, including four 30-mm. Aden guns. Ordnance: 4.1 tons. Range: some 1,850 miles.
Tu-16	This is a Soviet-built long-range strategic bomber, variants of which have been constructed for maritime reconnaissance, attack, and electronic intelligence purposes. Different versions carry the turbojet-powered airplane-type Kennel antishipping missile, the large standoff antishipping bomb, Kipper, and the rocket-powered Kelt missile. Additional armament includes 23-mm. cannons, bombs, and other air-to-surface antishipping missiles. Speed: 587 mph. Ordnance: 10 tons. Range (with maximum bomb load): 3,000 miles at 480 mph.; with 6,600 lbs. of bombs, 3,975 miles.
Mirage V	A ground-attack aircraft that can also be used as an interceptor. It is based on the Mirage III-E but can carry greater amounts of fuel and external ordnance than its predecessor. Its military load is like that of the Mirage III-E. Avionics include air-to-air interception radar, with an additional mode for control from the ground, and a sighting system giving air-to-air capabilities for cannons and missiles and an air-to-ground capability for dive bombing. Speed: Mach 2+. Ordnance: 4.4 tons. Combat radius: 400-805 miles.
A-4E	The A-4E fighter bomber is equipped with an angle-of-attack indicator, terrain clearance radar and a variety of optional warloads, such as Sidewinder infrared air-to-air missiles, Bullpup air-to-surface missiles, bombs, torpedoes, ground-attack gun pods, and countermeasures equipment. Maximum speed: 673 mph. Ordnance: 5 tons. Combat radius: 400-800 miles.
MiG-21	The MiG-21 is fitted with search-and-track plus warning radar and four Atoll air-to-air missiles, with a probable infrared guidance system similar to that of the American-made Sidewinder 1A. Maximum speed: Mach 2.1. Ordnance: .6 ton. Combat radius: 350 miles.

Source: *Jane's All the World's Aircraft, 1974-75, 1975-76,* and *1976-77.*

Table A-8

CHARACTERISTICS OF MAJOR HELICOPTERS

Type	Characteristics
Super Frelon (SA-321)	The French-made Super Frelon is a three-engined heavy-duty helicopter that comes in several versions, including one for ASW duties. It carries a crew of two plus twenty-seven to thirty troops and has a maximum TO weight of 28,600 lbs. It is equipped with a number of antisubmarine attack weapons, devices for minesweeping, and Exocet missiles for attacking surface ships. Speed: 171 mph. Range (ferry): 633 miles.
Bell 214A	A modern, American-built sixteen-seat utility helicopter. The 214A set altitude and time-to-height records in 1975. Maximum TO weight: 13,000 lbs. Cruising speed: 150 mph. Range: 299 miles. External load maximum TO weight: 15,000 lbs.
AB-205A	The AB-205A is an Italian- and American-made multipurpose helicopter similar to the UH-1D. It can carry up to fourteen passengers plus pilot and a variety of attachments including armament depending upon its role. TO weight: 10,500 lbs. Maximum speed: 138 mph. Range: 331 miles.
AB-212	A twin-engined Italian-American utility transport helicopter that carries up to fourteen passengers plus pilot. Cruising speed: 127 mph. Range (on one engine): 366 miles. A greatly modified naval model, the AB-212ASW, is designed for an ASW role. It carries Mk 44 or Mk 46 homing torpedoes, depth charges, or air-to-surface missiles. Maximum TO weight: 11,196 lbs. Maximum speed: 122 mph. Range (with auxiliary tanks): 414 miles.
S-65A	A U.S.-built turbine heavy assault all-weather transport helicopter which comes in several versions. One, the CH-53A, typically carries two jeeps, two Hawk missiles, or a 105-mm. howitzer. Another, the HH-53B/C is a heavy lift helicopter with various uses. Another, the CH-53D can be used for airborne minesweeping assignments. Maximum TO weight: 42,000 lbs. Maximum speed: 196 mph. Range: 257-540 miles.
KV-107/II	A Japanese-American twin-engined transport helicopter that comes in several models, variously suitable for airline use, troop transport, tactical cargo transport, mine countermeasures, long-range search and rescue. It carries three crew plus twenty-five passengers in its airline model. Maximum TO weight: 19,000 lbs. Maximum speed (at maximum TO weight): 168 mph. Range with 6,600 lb. payload (10 percent fuel reserve): 109 miles.

Type	Characteristics
Wasp (Westland HAS Mk1)	A British-built five/six seat, general-purpose helicopter which can carry an AS-12 air-to-surface missile. Maximum TO weight: 5,500 lbs. Maximum speed: 120 mph. Range: 270 miles.
Alouette III	A French general-purpose, seven-seat helicopter that comes in two main variants: a general-purpose armed reconnaissance and antitank version and an ASW version. The former can be equipped with a variety of weapons including a 20-mm. cannon, rockets, machine gun, and AS-11 and AS-12 wire-guided missiles. Tests have been completed demonstrating the successful use of HOT tube-launched, wire-guided antitank missiles. The ASW version carries Mk 44 homing torpedoes and a magnetic anomaly detector. For use against small surface craft such as torpedo boats, it carries AS-12 missiles. Maximum TO weight: 4,960 lbs. Speed: 136 mph. Range: 298-335 miles.
CH-47 Chinook	An American all-weather twin-engined medium transport helicopter capable of working under "severe combinations of altitude and temperature conditions." It carries two pilots, crew chief, and up to forty-four troops. Typical loads include a complete artillery section with crew and ammunition. All components of the Pershing missile system, for example, are transportable by Chinooks. Under various combinations of models and conditions: maximum TO weight: 28,400-46,000 lbs. Maximum speed: 127-190 mph. Mission radius: 23-115 miles. Maximum ferry range (internal and integral auxiliary fuel only): 962-1,400 miles.
S-61A and SH-3D (Sikorsky)	The S-61A is an American-built amphibious transport similar to the SH-3D Seaking which is the U.S. Navy's standard ASW helicopter. Both are twin-engined, amphibious, and have an all-weather capability. The S-61A carries twenty-six troops, while the SH-3D carries pilot, copilot, two sonar operators, and 840 lbs. of weapons including depth charges and homing torpedoes. Normal TO weights: S-61A: 20,500 lbs.; SH-3D (ASW): 18,626 lbs. Maximum speed: 166 mph. Range (with maximum fuel, 10 percent reserve): 625 miles.
UH-1D Iroquois	The U.S.-made Iroquois can carry a pilot plus eleven to fourteen troops. Maximum TO weight: 9,500 lbs. Maximum speed: 127 mph. Range (with maximum fuel, no allowances, no reserves at maximum weight): 318 miles.

Table A-8 (continued)

Type	Characteristics
AB-206A	The Italian- and American-built AB-206A seats four passengers in addition to the pilot and can carry various weapons. Maximum TO weight (external load): 3,350 lbs. Cruising speed: 130 mph. Range: 931 miles.
Mi-8	The Soviet-built Mi-8 carries two pilots and twenty-eight to thirty-two passengers. It can carry different weapons including rockets on external twin racks. Maximum TO weight: 26,455 lbs. Cruising speed: 112-140 mph. Range (cargo version with auxiliary fuel): 745 miles.
Mi-6 (Hook)	The Russian-made Mi-6 is a transport helicopter, which carries a crew of five and up to sixty-five passengers. It may be fitted with a gun of unknown caliber. Maximum weight: 93,700 lbs. Maximum cruising speed: 155 mph. Range (ferry): 900 miles.
Westland Seaking	An advanced British ASW helicopter with a capability for a number of other roles, such as search and rescue, tactical troop transport evacuation, cargo carrying, and long-range self-ferry. Seaking can carry four Mk 44 homing torpedoes or four Mk-11 depth charges. It can also carry Martel air-to-surface missiles. Maximum load capacity: 8,000 lbs. Speed: 143 mph. Ferry/transit range: 520 nm with standard fuel; 750 nm with auxiliary fuel.
SA-330 Puma (Aerospatiale/ Westland)	This is a French/British-made all-weather day or night transport helicopter. It carries up to three crew plus sixteen to twenty troops, 5,511 lbs. cargo internally and 606 lbs. cargo externally. Maximum TO weight: 14,770 lbs. Maximum speed: 174.5 mph. Maximum range (with standard fuel): 385 miles.

Source: *Jane's All the World's Aircraft, 1974-75, 1975-76,* and *1976-77.*

Table A-9
CHARACTERISTICS OF MAJOR TANKS

Type	Characteristics
T-62	This is believed to be standard equipment in the Soviet armored forces. It has a 115-mm. smoothbore gun and a top speed of about 30 mph. It can cross water up to about eighteen feet in depth and has night-vision equipment.
T-54/55	Some are still in service with the Soviet armored forces. This tank is equipped with a 100-mm. gun and has a road speed of about 30 mph. It can cross water up to about eighteen feet in depth and has night-vision equipment.
Pt-76	The Pt-76 is a light amphibious tank used as the main reconnaissance vehicle of the Soviet army. It is capable of operating in a fast-flowing river. It is considered mobile but has limitations as a fighting vehicle because its armor protection is less than that of other light tanks. This vehicle has a 76-mm. low-velocity gun and a road speed of about 25 mph. It apparently has no night-vision equipment.
M-60	The M-60 is currently a main battle tank of the U.S. army. It carries a 105-mm. high-velocity gun, has a top speed of about 30 mph, can cross water up to about thirteen feet in depth, and possesses night-vision equipment. Its cross-country mobility is said to be inferior to that of more modern European tanks.
M-48	The M-48 is the main tank armament of the U.S. Marine Corps. It has a 90-mm. M-41 gun and a road speed of about 30 mph. Night-vision equipment can be fitted.
T-59 (Chinese)	The Chinese T-59 is a modified variant of the Soviet T-54 tank without the gun stabilizer, infrared equipment and power traverse of the T-54. Since the gunner and the loader of the T-59 have hand traverse mechanisms, the tank has a poor rate of engagement and is effectively limited to engagement on a flat fire position. Although improvements may have been made on later models, those T-59s supplied to Pakistan suffer from these limitations.
T-62 (Chinese)	The T-62 is said to resemble a miniature T-59 and to carry an 85-mm. gun and a coaxial 7.62-mm. machine gun.
AMX-13	A French-built light tank that has been one of the most successful tanks of the postwar era. Continually manufactured in evolving models for twenty years, the AMX-13 originally carried a 75-mm. gun

Type	Characteristics
	but now may be fitted with one of 90 mm. or an electrically fired gun of 105 mm. It has great mobility and a low profile. An oscillating turret permits the use of an automatic loading device with a high rate of fire. The AMX-13 has an optimal range finder linked to a sight and laser range finder and infrared equipment for night use.
Vijayanta	Vijayanta (Victorious) is the Indian-manufactured version of the British-built Vickers main battle tank. This tank was designed to be a cheaper, more mobile, and lighter alternative to the Chieftain, the successor to Centurion. Weighing 37 tons, Vijayanta has a laser sight and a 105-mm. gun, and can wade in 2.2 meters of water.
M-47 Patton	The M-47 possesses a 90-mm. gun and stereoscopic range finder. No night capability. Wades in 1.2 meters of water.
Chieftain	Chieftain is the best tank in the inventories of Indian Ocean littoral states. A main battle (52.3 tons) tank, carrying a very accurate 120-mm. gun, it is designed with optimum protection of its turret. It uses a laser range finder, and it carries various infrared equipment for nighttime navigation, search, and targeting. It can wade in 5 meters of water.
Scorpion	The Scorpion is a British-made modern light tank with exceptional mobility on various terrains. Carrying a 76-mm. gun, Scorpion can cross water 1 meter deep and, with the aid of an inbuilt flotation screen, has the capability to swim inland waters.
AMX-30	AMX-30 is the lightest (36 tons) main battle tank, carrying a 105-mm. gun (designed primarily for anti-tank purposes). It is well protected because of its mobility, effective observation facilities, and inconspicuous silhouette as well as its laminated armor. Equipped with infrared searchlight and sights, it can wade in up to 4 meters of water.
Leopard	A German-built medium tank with exceptional mobility, and a powerful accurate quick-firing 105-mm. gun. Leopard has proved to be very reliable and easy to maintain. With the ability to wade in 4 meters of water, it is equipped with infrared searchlight, viewers, and sights for night use. Speed: 65 km/hr. Leopard has been built in three versions: ARV (armored recovery vehicle), CEV (combat engineer vehicle), and bridgelayer.

Source: *Jane's Weapons Systems 1976.*